HOW ARCHITECTS WRITE

This is the first writing reference book for designers. Whether you're an architect, landscape architect, interior designer, or an industrial designer, *How Architects Write* shows you the interdependence of writing and design. Authors Tom Spector and Rebecca Damron present typical writing assignments and explain principles of effective writing by including examples of good form and illustrating common pitfalls.

The book includes resources for how to write a thesis, designer's manifesto, statements of design intent, criticism, proposals, review statements, research reports, specifications, field reports, client communications, post-occupancy evaluations, and emailed meeting agendas so that you can navigate your career from school to the profession.

Tom Spector is a practicing architect and a professor at the Oklahoma State University School of Architecture.

Rebecca Damron is Assistant Professor of English and Director of the Writing Center at Oklahoma State University.

HOW ARCHITECTS WRITE

Tom Spector

and

Rebecca Damron

Routledge
Taylor & Francis Group

NEW YORK AND LONDON

First published 2013
by Routledge
711 Third Avenue, New York, NY 10017

Simultaneously published in the UK
by Routledge
2 Park Square, Milton Park, Abingdon, Oxon OX14 4RN

Routledge is an imprint of the Taylor & Francis Group, an informa business

Library of Congress Cataloging in Publication Data
Spector, Tom, 1957–
    How architects write/Tom Spector and Rebecca Damron.
    p. cm.
    Includes bibliographical references and index.
    1. Architectural writing.   I. Damron, Rebecca L.   II. Title.
    NA2540.S59 2012
    720.2 – dc23   2011041704

ISBN: 978-0-415-89106-6 (hbk)
ISBN: 978-0-415-89107-3 (pbk)
ISBN: 978-0-203-12218-1 (ebk)

Typeset in Galliard, Univers and Stone Sans
by Florence Production Ltd, Stoodleigh, Devon

Acquisition editor: Wendy Fuller
Project manager: Laura Williamson
Production editor: Gail Newton
Designer and typesetter: Florence Production Ltd

CONTENTS

IMAGE CREDITS

ACKNOWLEDGMENTS

This book began as a school task force investigation into architecture students' writing difficulties. We wish to thank our fellow task force members, Susan Bobo and Jeanne Homer, for their early research contributions and editorial input. We also wish to thank Michael Rabens and Moh Bilbeisi for their guidance, the students whose work has helped us illustrate types of writing exemplified throughout the book, to Steven Hopkins for early editorial and formatting assistance, and to Ivory Lin for painstakingly checking source materials for documentation purposes. Thanks to Wendy Fuller and Laura Williamson at Routledge for their encouragement and editorial guidance. We are grateful to our families for providing the emotional support that helped us persevere through the writing of this book.

HOW (AND WHY) ARCHITECTS WRITE

Now if it were asked: "Do you have the thought before finding the expression?" what would one have to reply? And what, to the question: "What did the thought consist in, as it existed before its expression?"

(Ludwig Wittgenstein, philosopher)[1]

Architects often finish their sentences with a sketch.

(Peter Medway, applied linguist)[2]

THE NEED FOR CLEAR WRITING

Clarity. If the objectives of this handbook could be boiled down to a single watchword, this would be it. The objective of writing clearly has so many dimensions—clarity of intent, clarity of expression, clarity of audience—it can seem an overwhelming task at first. Fortunately, the task becomes less formidable when broken down into its four constituent parts (Figure 1.1). Good writers have sufficient command of their *subject matter* to convey confidence that they know what they are talking about. Their use of language is both clear and appropriate—they understand the *rhetorical standards* expected of them. They have a firm grasp on their *writing process*—

Subject Matter Knowledge

Building: Hemispheric
Location: City of Arts and Sciences,
   Valencia, Spain
Architect: Santiago Calatrava
Date: 1998

Rhetorical Knowledge

Daniel Libeskind's Jewish Museum
in Berlin seeks to convey emotions
of horror and moral outrage to the
Holocaust in a museum
experience. . . .

FIGURE 1.1 Writing's four knowledge types

Writing Process Knowledge

Field notes, Feb. 22:

Steel erected to 45th floor
Electrical service entry discussed
Membrane roof installed on
    building 1
Curtainwall mock-up panel
    reviewed
Retaining wall stabilized
Elevator shaft wall #2 corrected
Prefabricated steel stairs ordered

Genre Knowledge

Evolution of High-Tech:

1. Early Milestones
a. Pompidou Center
b. James Stirling's
    buildings in the UK
2. High-Tech goes
    mainstream
a. Norman Foster

not only mastery of the mechanics, grammar, and self-editing emphasized in freshman composition, but also of the steps required to, for example, organize their observations into reports. And they have clarified the expectations of their audience; that is to say, they understand the demands of the *genre* in which they are writing.

By mastering the elements of clear architectural writing —gaining command over the subject matter, employing appropriate rhetorical standards, establishing efficient processes, and understanding the demands of the different writing genres—students and practitioners will not only become better writers but will also make themselves better architects.

When the role of writing in architectural production was used primarily to explain a design that was already conceived visually, then the written word could be relegated to an ornamental role at the tail end of a linear process (Figure 1.2). Writing happened after all the really interesting work was done. But this conception is long out of date.

Writing doesn't just record what has already been done; it is part of the doing. What linguist Peter Medway discovered by observing both architectural practitioners and students was the *fluidity* with which architects must move between the graphic, oral, and written modes when developing and communicating design intent. This is the observation his quote at the beginning of the chapter is meant to convey. After observing architects at work in a number of different situations, he offers, "We are surprised and impressed by the *linguistic* virtuosity called for in the job."[3] Yes, sentences do end in sketches, but by the same token, sketches are illuminated by sentences. The design moves forward, not linearly, but iteratively as the designer gropes toward a desired future state of affairs. It gains authority as the mind incorporates information from a variety of sources. If design is allowed to be about more than the creation of geometric form, then a fluid conception which places design at the center of an activity informed by graphic, oral, and written modes is a more adequate representation.

If the linear conception of writing's role in architecture was ever adequate, it certainly is not now. Both the increasingly collaborative environment of the construction economy and the

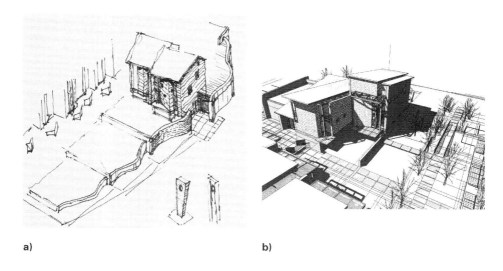

a)   b)

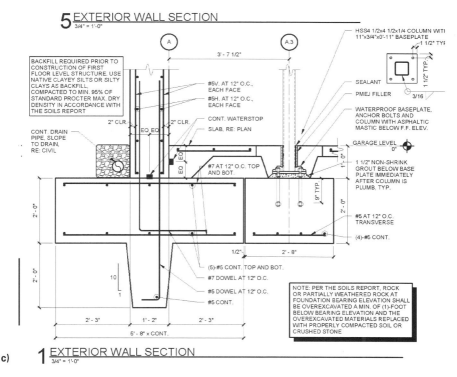

c)

FIGURE 1.2 Writing's role in the linear view: (a) a design is conceived in models, drawings, and sketches; (b) it is presented with advanced graphics and oral explanation; (c) instructions are communicated via 2-D graphics and writing

technological advances in the design process have placed a premium on architects' ability to write to be effective on the job. Whereas at one time architects might have conceived of themselves as visual artists handing-off their designs for others to figure out how to build, today they are more likely to be at the center of an integrated team needing someone to organize its intense communication needs. These days, the value of one's investments may fade, but emails are forever. Litigation—and preventing it—is heavily dependent on crisp, clear writing. Nor is effective writing only business-oriented. No one achieves stature in the profession without at least one monograph explaining the firm's design thinking. Press and criticism are as important as ever for building a critical reputation. Meanwhile, the explosion of information that can now be brought to bear on a building design means that someone must be able to manage and organize it, and the logical center of the design process resides with the persons charged with bringing the diverse sources of information together. To exploit the opportunities the information age presents, architects must be able to write well, edit, and integrate the information generated by others into a coherent whole. The erosion of the concept of the architect as Master Builder is disappearing into that of the architect as Master of Information. This new role is not a demotion but it does signify a shift in how the world is pressing architects to think about design. In this emerging model, the design itself is usefully understood as existing either suspended at the center of a web of diverse information, or else is actually the sum of all the information that comes to bear on it. Architectural form emerges out of and becomes part of the sea of relevant information, which includes the written word. Taken together, these developments make the need for achieving clarity in one's writing all the more urgent, and central.

FOUR TYPES OF WRITING KNOWLEDGE: SUBJECT MATTER, RHETORICAL, PROCESS, AND GENRE

Think of the four aspects of clear writing as four different types of knowledge. Where and how are they transmitted? As it turns out, the majority must come from within one's chosen discipline and cannot be subcontracted out to the English department with any expectation of success. Most of the work students do to improve their writing will necessarily come from within the architecture school curriculum. This is why the chapters in this book are organized around the typical writing tasks encountered as one progresses through school.

Subject Matter Knowledge

It is easy to see how one would be unable to think, much less write, perceptively within the field of architecture in the absence of such discipline-specific subject matter knowledge as architecture history, construction technology, and contractual relationships. By analyzing a fifth-year undergraduate student's architectural design thesis, Medway saw the process of a student's move into "architectural thinking" through a trajectory that included alternations of drawing and writing, a process that resulted in writing functioning as a design tool.[4] In doing so, he demonstrated that students can never fully compensate for a spotty architecture vocabulary with, say, formal virtuosity because subject matter knowledge is so fundamental. Much of the writing done in architecture school is to demonstrate that one has assimilated and can synthesize subject matter information into one's observations (Chapters 2 and 6) and one's understanding of history (Chapters 3 and 7, especially).

FIGURE 1.3 Subject Matter Knowledge

Rhetorical Knowledge

Some rhetorical knowledge does apply across disciplines, but only the most basic rhetorical elements of argumentation and logic can be effectively installed by outsiders. To see why this is so, consider Medway's contention that design itself is rhetorical in nature and, thus, schools of architecture teach students how to argue. This argumentative education is not only learned through the oral elements of crits or reviews, but also in the process of design itself: "Buildings that lack a 'proposition' or idea . . . are ineffective (as is criticism that evades these issues)."[5] He also sees broader implications for understanding the role of rhetoric in architecture: the propositional content of design is a crucial element enabling students to make rational and reasonable decisions as their designs progress. Students who are unable to adequately theme and structure their arguments have a poor grasp of just the sort of knowledge that, if left uncorrected, will ultimately weaken the propositional content of their designs. When the propositional content is vague, ill-formed,

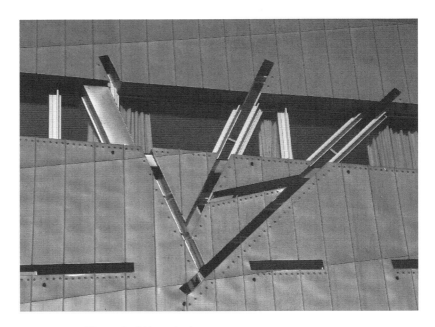

FIGURE 1.4 Rhetorical Knowledge

or inarticulate, design judgment will all too easily be reduced to the low common denominators of "it works" or "it looks good." The subject of rhetorical knowledge will receive its most complete treatment in Chapters 3 and 4.

Writing Process Knowledge

Writing process knowledge is procedural knowledge that helps the writer move through the writing task. Student problems such as poor writing mechanics and grammar take their toll here and this is the

FIGURE 1.5 Writing Process Knowledge

one type of knowledge that is perhaps rightfully the realm of the English department and freshman composition. As noted earlier, attention to these processes is important for effective communication, and students must learn to attend to their own editing processes. But, as the writing tasks become more specific to the discipline, once again their instruction should shift to architecture school and practice because writing process knowledge is so immensely affected by the material and social context in which the writing task takes place. Synthesizing and relaying the results of one's research into new materials, technologies, parameters and constraints is beholden to establishing effective writing processes. How to accomplish the effective communication of one's research will be explained in Chapter 5. Even a seemingly straightforward task, such as composing a field report (Chapter 6) requires that an architect must know how observations become instructions—the architect arrives at the site with a concept in mind of the desired outcome (the quality of the building); then compares observed progress with the conception (note-taking on the observations), reconciling observations with preconceptions; and finally, through writing, he or she explains the thought processes used to arrive at decisions. The process of note-taking, reconciling those notes, and then writing the final report illustrates the indispensability of possessing an understanding of a writing process to the successful realization of one's design ideas.

Genre Knowledge

Architectural writing incorporates a number of unique genres. In essence, the chapters are separated by the genres they analyze. These genres are typically highly structured, conventionalized forms that are created and maintained by experienced members of the community who transmit their genre knowledge to its novices. Indeed, a lack of genre knowledge helps signal the difference in understanding between novice and established architects even when they apparently have similar levels of technical knowledge. These differences are apparent even between beginning and advanced students in the design studio. The unique institution of the architect's journal (Chapter 2) is a case in point. Medway studied architecture students' sketchbooks to determine their function as a genre. The function of the sketchbooks varied from non-work related uses to recording and preserving observations, as well as aids to thinking, learning, and preparing for actions. Because they are never limited to purely sketching, journals exemplify the need for fluidity between the verbal and visual, even for what is ostensibly an audience of one. While presumably not intended for an external audience, these notebooks did, according to Medway, participate in social action, a criterion of a genre. Genre knowledge is what allows architects to know how to write effectively for their different audiences. The unfortunate phenomenon of "Archispeak" or "Archibabble" occurs when they fail to appreciate the boundaries of these audiences and write for a community of, say, newspaper readers as if it were a group that would read an architects' journal. This discriminating function of genres is best appreciated in conjunction with the important concept of a *discourse community*.

FIGURE 1.6 Genre Knowledge

ARCHITECTS' TWO DISCOURSE COMMUNITIES

When authors begin to master the elements of clear writing, not only do they express their thoughts more effectively (as wonderful as this is) but they also begin to take their place in a larger world of writers. Their effective writing allows them to both participate in and add to the existing knowledge in their *discourse community*. A writer's discourse community includes, but is greater than, the immediate audience for any given piece of writing. A discourse community is a group of people that develops a sense of identity primarily through the writing of and for its members. Through reading one comes to understand a community; through writing one participates in it. Though the four constituent parts of clear writing apply to any discourse community, each community of writers and readers develops unique and characteristic formats for its writing; it acquires its own technical language that helps writers add precision and brevity to their communications, the community evolves its own standards for writing well, and its writers know with a high degree of specificity who they are writing for.

In the field of architecture, it is important to understand at the outset that the profession spans two different discourse communities with their own distinct standards and needs: an *internal* discourse with which architects communicate with fellow architects, educators, critics, and theorists of various stripes in the ongoing effort to improve and redefine the discipline; and an *external* discourse with such "outsiders" as clients, engineers, contractors, building officials, and the public with whom architects must cooperate for the actual production of buildings (Figure 1.7).

Both communities are indispensable to the field. Successful architectural practitioners will be fluent in both kinds of discourse and they will know when one or the other is appropriate. Chapters 2 and 3 analyze forms of writing oriented primarily for architecture's internal audience, while 4, 5, and 6 are concerned primarily with architects' communication with the world external to the discipline. Chapters 7 and 8, then, culminate with a return to writing at a more advanced level of synthesis for an internal audience.

a) Internal

b) External

FIGURE 1.7 (a) Practice spans architecture's internal discourse (fellow architects, educators, trade journals, critics) and (b) its external discourse (engineers, contractors, clients, building officials, the public)

WRITING WELL MAKES YOU SMARTER

Students entering architecture school often cite the ability to be creative while earning a reasonable living as a prime motivator for choosing architecture. But what many come to find over time is that, while the qualities inspiring that initial motivation are true as far as they go, what they could not appreciate until they had been in school for a while is how *engrossing* architecture is. Its study and design engage all one's mental processes at a very high level. Both in school and on the job, one experiences a constant pushing against one's intellectual limitations. As architects struggle to find the most penetrating expression of their design thinking, the mind bootstraps increasingly sophisticated thoughts on the available intellectual resources. Wittgenstein's elegantly stated question at the beginning of the chapter is meant to illustrate the wonder and fragility of this transcendence beyond the already-known; and how the horizons of thought are determined by the ability to express oneself. Of all the venues for recording and transmitting thought, for creating communities of thinkers, and for putting together new thoughts in flashes of creativity, writing is the most versatile.

This book is envisioned as a handy reference that will follow the standard architectural curriculum and help guide students through its writing component. Though it is organized to track the typical assignments students encounter as they move up and through the curriculum, we also hope practitioners will find it to be a ready reference to help them clarify why architects write and who architects are writing for. Filled with practical advice for clearer writing, its ultimate goal is to enable more moments of transcendence of one's previous limitations.

DESIGN JOURNALS

Keeping a design journal is fundamental to an ongoing practice of writing and an important source of ideas for any writing or design project on which you might wish to embark. In essence, it is writing done for yourself on your own time. The design journal is different from other kinds of writing you will do because the purpose is not always immediately evident, the content is less important than the sketching and writing process, and there is no specific audience. These qualities may make you think that the design journal is a waste of time, but many designers consider keeping a journal in which to record observations and ideas an indispensable aid to their work.

The design journal is a space for you to record your observations, analyze your sketches, organize your thoughts, and refine your ideas. In this way the design journal becomes a source of reflection, which is an important aspect of the design process. Donald Schön calls design a "reflective conversation with the situation."[1] This means that design is not a single-step process, but an ongoing dialogue to match a plan with the material conditions of the design context. The design journal represents this kind of dialogue because it includes a "conversation" between the text and the image. Notice in the following series of images how the conversation develops. It becomes more rich and meaningful as the written elements are added to the image.

USING THE DESIGN JOURNAL: AN EXAMPLE

The images in Figures 2.1, 2.2, and 2.3 show the evolution of a sketch into a useful journal entry. The first presents an image alone (Figure 2.1). This image certainly does convey information on its own and without words, but what use can be made of it? What lessons or ideas can be had from it?

FIGURE 2.1

The second panel presents the image with notations (Figure 2.2). These notations aid memory and help draw the author's attention to things that he or she thought important at the time, or that perhaps were not well described by the image alone.

FIGURE 2.2

The author uses notations and lists here, which certainly help organize his or her thoughts about the thing described. Yet they still do not explain what the designer was hoping to capture in the scene. The designer might be thinking, "Yes, it appears to be a nice-looking stone building with Gothic details, but what about it?"

The third panel shows the annotated image with the addition of a complete sentence (Figure 2.3). Sentences are the crucial addition which enable the designer to record not only the thing observed but also what ideas or lessons occurred to him or her at the time. Only with the addition of sentences do we begin

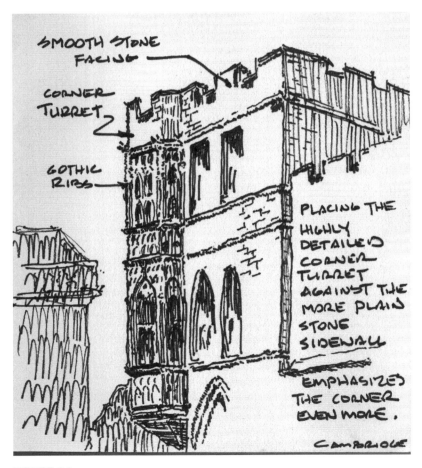

FIGURE 2.3

to know why the author recorded the image to begin with or what it was about the image that he or she wanted to recall at some future date. The sentence, it turns out, is the basic unit of design communication.

Note that the sentence in the third panel is not merely declarative in the form of "I like this!" or "This is a really pretty building in Cambridge." Neither does it seek to relate merely factual information such as, "This building belongs to Gonville and Caius College." Instead, it seeks to record a discovery: a lesson learned. These are the sorts of thoughts designers might find useful in the future if, for instance, they ever find themselves needing to emphasize an important corner condition.

THE IMPORTANCE OF A DESIGN JOURNAL

A journal, while initially private, needs to serve the designer's ultimate goal of communicating design ideas to others. It is not a "journal" in the sense of a daily diary, which is entirely private and personal, nor is it purely a sketchbook where the image is the end product. Some of the observations and ideas that begin as journal entries will eventually be incorporated in design work presented to others. Effective journaling, therefore, sets the stage for effective communication later.

The design journal contains a record that allows you to remember what your thought processes were when you sketched a particular item, and allows you to review and reflect on whether your observations fit with your overall design plan. The design journal can assist this process in three important ways:

- Problem setting and problem solving
- Developing and clarifying thoughts
- Practicing

Each of these provides the designer with tools for deepening his or her thinking about a project, and engaging in the process in individual ways that will lead to professional insights.

Problem Setting and Problem Solving

> When a design problem is so overwhelming as to be nearly
> paralyzing, don't wait for clarity to arrive before beginning to
> draw. Drawing is not simply a way of depicting a design
> solution; it is itself a way of learning about the problem you
> are trying to solve.
>
> (Matthew Frederick, architect and instructor)[2]

> The journal contains solutions to all the problems that arise in
> the course of the writing. Sometimes the breakthroughs are
> sudden; more often the answers are painstakingly arrived at
> through trial and error.
>
> (Sue Grafton, crime novelist)[3]

Sometimes, simply identifying the problem or asking the right
questions that can help you identify problems is where you need to
start. The design journal is a space where you can do this by
brainstorming, asking questions, and pinpointing issues that will help
name the problem and give you a proper frame within which to
work. In the quote at the beginning of this section, Grafton
emphasizes the notion that the act of writing itself can yield
solutions, but we have to be persistent. Together, drawing and
writing in the design notebook can provide a powerful space for the
designer to work through the design process.

Take a look at the following journal entry entitled
"Redrock" (Figure 2.4) to see how the designer uses text and image
to define and illustrate a problem.

The designer employs a plan view to help him analyze what
he sees as a disconnect between high-quality food and a poorly
organized space. The plan view illustrates the traffic flow problems
within the space and simultaneously describes the experience with
words. A single paragraph is enough to allow the designer to analyze
the problem and draw some conclusions. Text and image combine to
create a descriptive force neither could manage alone. Because the
designer has successfully analyzed the traffic flow problems at this
restaurant, in the future, the designer can avoid similar planning
difficulties.

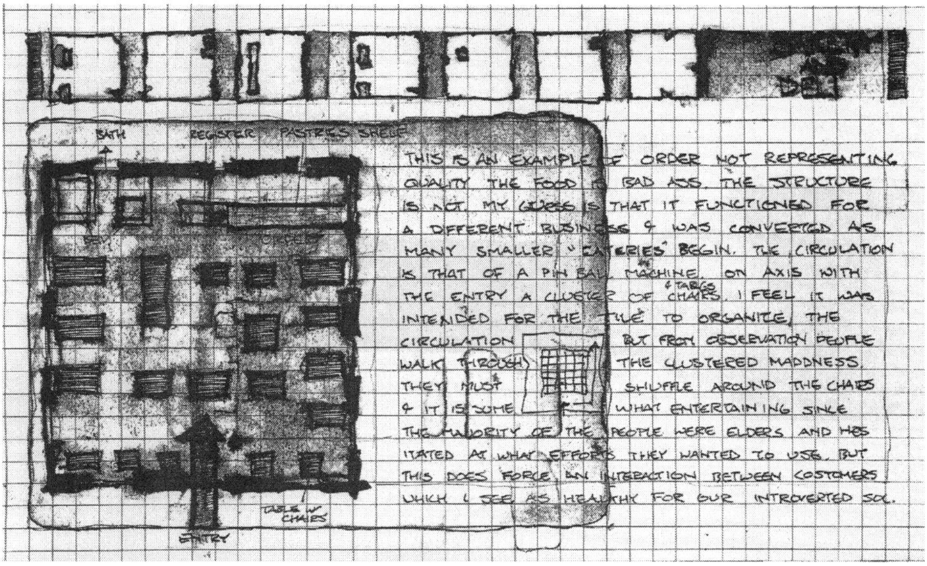
BATH
REGISTER
ENTRY
THIS IS AN EXAMPLE OF ORDER NOT REPRESENTING
QUALITY THE FOOD IS BAD ASS. THE STRUCTURE
IS NOT. MY GUESS IS THAT IT FUNCTIONED FOR
A DIFFERENT BUSINESS & WAS CONVERTED AS
MANY SMALLER "EATERIES" BEGIN. THE CIRCULATION
IS THAT OF A PIN BALL MACHINE. ON AXIS WITH
THE ENTRY A CLUSTER OF CHAIRS. I FEEL IT WAS
INTENDED FOR THE TILE TO ORGANIZE THE
CIRCULATION BUT FROM OBSERVATION PEOPLE
WALK THROUGH THE CLUSTERED MADDNESS.
THEY MUST SHUFFLE AROUND THE CHAIRS
& IT IS SOME WHAT ENTERTAINING SINCE
THE MAJORITY OF THE PEOPLE WERE ELDERS AND HES
ITATED AT WHAT EFFORTS THEY WANTED TO USE. BUT
THIS DOES FORCE AN INTERACTION BETWEEN COSTOMERS
WHICH I SEE AS HEALTHY FOR OUR INTROVERTED SOC.

FIGURE 2.4 Redrock

Developing and Clarifying Thoughts

Well-known artists, architects, and designers such as Leonardo DaVinci and Le Corbusier kept journals. We can see development in their thinking by looking at their texts.

The next example shows how the image and the text work together to help the student develop some broader ideas about the architecture in the text.

In "Exercise One" (Figure 2.5), a student is developing detailed thoughts by using the text as mutually supportive with the image rather than merely supplementing the image. The designer's thoughts about the evolution of architectural form are illustrated by the sketch. In particular, we see that the author is thinking about how a given set of forms can be interpreted as both religious and governmental architecture. The image illustrates this idea well: The building depicted could easily be either. By allowing the text and image to be equally important in this journal entry, the designer is allowing himself to record and reflect on sophisticated concepts;

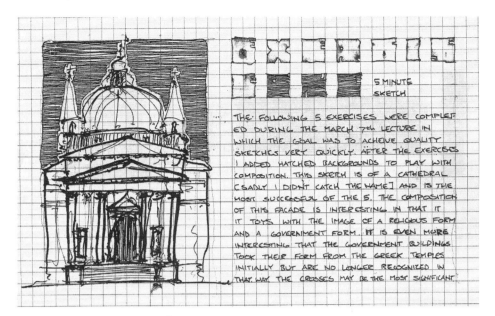

FIGURE 2.5 Exercise One

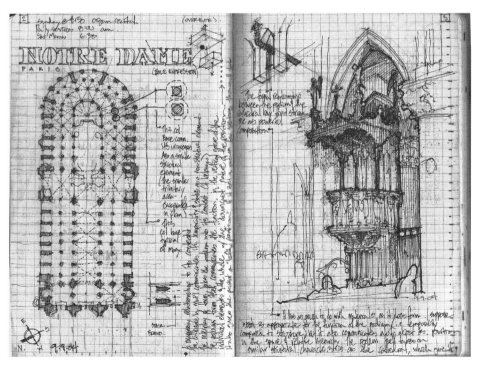

FIGURE 2.6 Notre Dame

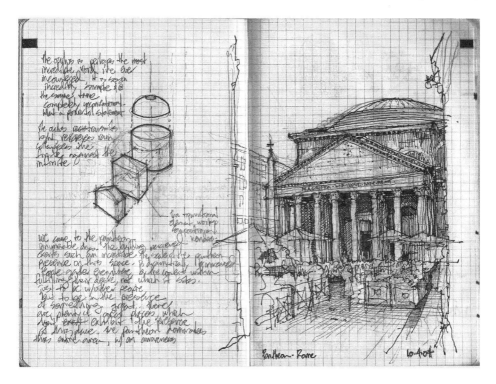

FIGURE 2.7 Pantheon

in this case, the subtle differences that lead to different perceptions of a building's role in the community.

In the journal entry "Notre Dame" (Figure 2.6), the interlacing of text and images is more complex and more powerful still. Here the designer sketches the entire plan of the great Paris cathedral, isolates details of the piers and the entry, and then pays special attention to the pulpit. He writes, "The formal relationship between the podium and the cathedral bay first struck me as powerful composition," and illustrates what he means with a diagram above and to the left. Perhaps realizing he has yet to come to grips with what it is about the composition that he finds powerful, he continues at the bottom of the page: "It has as much to do with materials as it does form. I suppose wood is appropriate for the function of the podium (i.e. temporality compared to the structure) but it also communicates a lot about its position in the space and relative hierarchy." Note that text and images are freely scattered about the two-page spread but are keyed into one another.

In the journal entry "Pantheon" (Figure 2.7), the designer creates a simple volumetric diagram accompanying the perspective sketch to document the discovery that the building is not simply a classical porch attached to a drum, but that an intermediate prismatic volume transitions between the two. He writes, "The transitional element works wonders," and points to it with a leader line. The author pays attention to his own subjective impressions and his reflection on them to fill-out the entry. He notes that he returned to the Pantheon repeatedly during his visit to Rome to "be in the presence of something great."

Practicing

The habit of sketching and writing takes time to develop, and both of these skills become better with extensive practice. Think of keeping a journal as daily practice. Like any exercise, it will provide long-term benefits to your drawing, your writing, and your thinking. In his book *Graphic Journaling*, Moh'd Bilbeisi says the journal is a "scratchpad for the brain."[4] If you are nervous or uneasy about starting a design journal, perhaps thinking of it as a scratchpad will help: a place you can dash off a thought, where there is no pressure to do something perfectly. It is your practice space. It may be difficult to start actually sketching or writing, and, more than likely, it will be neither good nor pretty. However, persistence is important, and over time you will notice differences.

One more valuable aspect of the design journal is that it provides a space in which you can rehearse the language and argumentation you will use for desk crits or oral presentations of your design. Many students find that putting their thoughts down on paper before doing an oral presentation can assist them in finding the right words and organization.

The following list here includes some suggestions to get you started and keep you going with your practice. This list is by no means exhaustive, but these are common journaling practices. Over time, you will find what works best for you and for the types of projects you engage in.

Freewriting. This is a kind of flow-of-consciousness writing in which you write whatever comes into your head. You keep the pen to the paper and just keep writing. This practice can help you generate ideas if your are at a loss at where to start with a design or if you have a sketch, but have no idea what to say about it. This practice helps you get started and helps your fluency in writing, especially if writing is something that does not come easy for you.

Focused Freewriting. In this practice, you would start with a prompt of some sort to generate the flow-of-consciousness writing. For example, you might have just learned about a certain concept in a lecture and have created a sketch, but want to figure out how that concept might apply to your image. Write whatever you know about that concept next to the image, and see where your brain takes you.

Lists. Lists are something we do everyday—To Do lists, grocery lists, etc. You can use lists to start generating your thoughts. For example, you could write a list next to your sketch of everything you know about a particular image.

Dialogue. Usually writers will use this strategy to develop various perspectives by putting people in conversation with each other. For this exercise, you could write an imaginary conversation with your instructor about a design and ask questions such as, "What would he or she say about it?" Or, you could put yourself in conversation with a famous designer and ask, "How would he or she see what you have done?" This exercise also helps us get some distance from what we are working on.

Metaphor. Metaphors map one thing onto another. For example, the expression "life is a journey" maps the abstract concept of life onto the more concrete process of a journey. Find a metaphor for your sketch or your design process and follow that metaphor with all of its implications to find fresh ways of thinking about your design, or the problems that you encounter.

Reflection. A valuable part of the journaling process is reviewing what you have written and reflecting on it. Every so often, look back at your journal entries and write something about what is happening in those entries. What have you learned? What is similar or different about the sketches, the writing or the interaction between the two? Doing this kind of reflection will help you discover your own voice or style and help identify areas in which you would like to grow.

THE TOOLS OF THE DESIGN JOURNAL

Now that you have some background for the benefits of keeping a journal and are convinced, we hope, that you would like to begin your own, you need to think about the tools of journaling. We will not go into great detail, but will give some guidelines to think about when choosing materials. We encourage you to experiment. It is fun and worthwhile to find what fits your style.

The two major items you will need are a writing instrument and a notebook. Determine whether a pen or a pencil works for you, and think about the advantages and disadvantages of each for the kinds of drawing and writing you will want to do. In addition, some journal keepers find that adding color is important, so markers or watercolors may be something to add to your repertoire. This is a very personal decision—you must be comfortable enough with your materials to want to use them frequently, and they must function well for your particular needs.

One thing to keep in mind when choosing your tools is their portability. As a designer and a journal keeper, you will probably want to record your observations of an environment in which you find yourself, and will need to have your tools handy. In addition, materials should be functional and durable. Do not get caught trying to capture an image or thought and have your tools fail you.

These days, there are many types of notebooks to choose from: fancy leather-bound journals, spiral-bound sketchbooks, and others. Consider the quality of the paper and choose what will work best for what you primarily want to do in the journal. For example, if you want to use watercolors, get a journal that has paper that will not curl up when it gets wet. If you carry your notebook with you, it will need to be tough enough to stand up to daily routine. Also, you will want to determine if blank pages, lined pages or pages with gridlines work best.

Organizing Your Journal

Finally, there are many ways that journal keepers have developed to organize their information. For example, they might include page numbers and titles for journal entries and include those titles in a table of contents at the front of the journal, or index particular concepts at the end of the journal. You could make dual use of the journal: from the front, you could do your regular sketching and writing, and then turn it over and, from the back of the journal, reflect on entries or write definitions, notes, or ideas for more entries. Again, there are no set rules because this is your space.

We hope that you will take advantage of the design journal in order to facilitate your own growth as a writer, sketcher, thinker, and designer. We know that as you develop your own journaling habits and skills, you will discover an indispensable tool for your design process that helps your development as a design professional. We are convinced that the sketch and the written word work together to deepen your understanding of design. We are going to leave you with a challenge that Andrea Ponsi took, which resulted in his lovely, thoughtful book *Florence: A Map of Perceptions*:

> Some years ago, during a hot, deserted August, I purposely left my usual watercolors sketchbook at home and decided to wander around Florence equipped with only a notebook and pen. I wanted to verify the power of the word, as opposed to drawing, to describe the city. The result of that initial experiment is this little book.
>
> The fact is that my interest as an architect has always been focused on representing the city by means of drawing,

whether from life or from memory. Like thin, flexible mirrors, the pages of this book reflect writings and drawings back and forth to each other, letting a mutual echo expand between them.

Readers will find evident convergences or inexplicable contradictions between these two *modi operandi*: I leave the judgment up to them. As far as I am concerned, the question is still open: Which of the two descriptions of the city is more pleasing, closer to reality, more capable of stimulating the imagination, the drawn or the written? To tell the truth, I would like not to have to choose, but to go on exploring, contemporaneously, both of these boundless territories.[5]

Take Ponsi's question and explore it. The drawing and the writing have the capacity to work together—and apart—in ways that can spark our creativity and imagination, but also provide structure for thinking and drawing. As we indicated at the beginning of this chapter, a habit of journaling will not always directly translate into your other writing projects. However, it will provide a space for you to try out ideas, develop those ideas, solve design problems, rehearse your language, and prepare you for the work of other writing assignments that are more focused on specific purposes, audiences, and structures.

To get you started as a design journal-keeper we have developed some exercises.

1. After purchasing your tools, spend a week trying the six suggested practices on pages 25–26. Then, answer the following questions (on a page in your journal!).

    a Which of the practices was most comfortable?

    b Which was the most difficult?

    c What was the context for each practice? Where and when did you do the practice and with what kind of image did you pair the writing?

    d Which ones would you use again? Why or why not?

2. Go through the process that we did earlier in the chapter:

    a Sketch an image

    b Add words

    c Add sentences

    Then write a paragraph that pulls the words and the sentences together.

3. As you begin a journal entry, think about how you might want the relationship between the image and the written text to work. Ask yourself the following questions:

    a How much text will I need?

    b What will the relationship between the text and the image be?

    c How will the page(s) look when I am finished?

4. Conversely, don't think about the relationship between an image and the text as you are doing the journal entry, but go back when you are finished and ask about the relationship between the two and whether they create an effective conversation.

exercises

5. Write down some concepts from a course lecture. Choose one, write the concept as the title for a journal entry and then sketch and write to that concept.

6. Sometimes it's hard to write details. Take one of your sketches and list all the details you see in the sketch.

7. Try to do what the student in Figure 2.5 "Exercise One" did: create a mutually supportive relationship between the image and the written text about an idea that you want to explore.

HISTORY TERM PAPERS

The assignment of writing a history term paper will likely be your first occasion to draw from all four types of knowledge in one assignment. It demonstrates that you understand the meaning of and are capable of an in-depth analysis of architectural matters—especially their cultural importance. It also shows that you are capable of writing in a way that meets the genre requirements of the field. To adequately discharge these requirements will require you to fine-tune your process and sharpen your rhetorical skills. Thus, writing the paper fulfills several educational requirements in your progress through school and into the profession. It is likely to be your initiation into participating in architecture's internal discourse.

But, perhaps of even more immediate importance, it demonstrates that you are capable of assembling propositional thoughts concerning architecture, its place in the wider scope of life, its internal development over time, and how its current concerns have come to be. Honing this important skill will positively influence your design skills—especially the ability to create buildings fully relevant to contemporary culture. A propositional thought is characterized by an initial speculative idea that is then applied to and tested against a body of knowledge. If you can begin the history term paper with a curiosity about a subject or with a question, then you are probably on the right track. If, on the other hand, you find yourself unable to generate any curiosity or questions about matters in architectural history, then you are likely ill-matched to the field.

Architecture is soaked to the bone in its own history; anyone who finds it uninteresting is crippled from the beginning in his or her own work. The skill of applying propositional thought to architectural history is the generating element of progress in the field. Facility in the skill, then, of generating interesting propositions can hardly be overestimated in importance. As with any skill—a good backhand in tennis, making a soufflé, speaking in public—it can be learned, internalized, and eventually made to feel natural. The more specific term for the type of propositional statement writers apply to a history term paper is the *thesis statement*.

The type of writing we address in this chapter will be most relevant in the context of your academic writing. However, this does not mean the skills that you learn from writing history—such as writing analytically or developing an argument—will not be helpful to you as a practicing architect or graduate student.

HOW TO BEGIN

First and foremost, read the assignment. What is the instructor asking you to do? You may be asked, for example, to describe buildings or summarize others' views, but most of the time you will be asked to analyze or argue a point about buildings, or an historical perspective or a particular view of an architect, scholar or historian. You may be asked to analyze what a building means, or discuss how buildings might reflect some cultural or architectural context. You might just need to narrate, or tell the story, of a building. This entails more than just a passing relationship with the material you will be reviewing to include in your paper. You will need to develop within yourself a working familiarity with your chosen topic.

For example, if you were to receive an assignment to write a paper about skyscrapers (Figure 3.1) such as the following:

Your assignment is to conduct research on a topic related to the history of skyscrapers between 1850 and the present. Your first task is to choose a topic. You may choose as your subject a single work of architecture (executed or projected),

FIGURE 3.1 8 Spruce Street, New York, Gehry Architects

a selected group of related works, the work of a single architect or architectural firm, theoretical writings, or any specific theme related to the history of skyscrapers. It is suggested, but not required, that you concentrate on works created before 1990, as there is more literature available on these buildings than on more recent developments.[1]

How would you go about analyzing this assignment in order to write about it? Three key terms you will want to focus on are *research*, *history*, and *between 1850 and the present*. So the topic of skyscrapers must be researched, which means going to other sources. Also, it is a history paper with a specific time period identified, which helps you focus your research. The next few sentences of the assignment help narrow down how the instructor wants to focus on this history of skyscrapers, and in this case, you have several choices. Whatever option you choose will determine how you research the paper, what kinds of evidence you will use to support your claims, and ultimately how you will organize your research and write the paper.

WRITING A THESIS STATEMENT

Your paper needs to have a central idea. This is where the importance of having a thesis statement emerges. In the case of a history paper, the thesis statement should consist of a sentence or two that indicate your paper's central claim.

Read through this paragraph from an article in the *Journal of the Society of Architectural Historians* by Elizabeth Kryder-Reid in which she is discussing the importance of mission gardens of California. The sentences have been numbered for ease of discussion.

1) While the history of the mission buildings is relatively well documented, the associated landscapes have received much less scrutiny. 2) Despite this neglect, the "mission gardens" have been a formative part of the public reception of the sites, whose symbolism and meaning must be considered in the

broader contexts of California historical and visual practices. 3) Among these iconic landscapes, Mission Santa Barbara exerted a seminal influence and was the archetypal mission garden. 4) The garden's design and reception were framed by contests for social and political hegemony, out of which it emerged as a central symbol of California's valorized colonial past.[2]

This paragraph is the third in the article. Kryder-Reid began by giving background to mission buildings, which are a much more familiar subject of study, in the first two paragraphs. As we can see in sentence 1), she is creating a transition to mission gardens by moving from mission buildings in the first part of the sentence to "landscapes" in the second part of the sentence. She is also establishing a gap in the scholarship, which her work will fill in this article. These gaps in scholarship are the norm for professional academics, who are extending knowledge in the field, but you will not be required to provide a gap in your paper. However, the gap helps establish the "so what" of the paper. Why would the reader be interested in this topic? This is a place where you can provide your instructor with the "so what" of your paper. Why was this topic of interest to you? She continues on more strongly in sentence 2) to emphasize the importance of this topic and at the same time she is narrowing the topic from "landscape" to the more specific precise term for her purposes, "mission gardens" in this sentence. She narrows the focus of her study to a particular mission garden, the Mission Santa Barbara in sentence 3), and then in sentence 4) she gives us the central idea: that mission gardens played a larger societal and historical role than is usually identified. As you can see, Kryder-Reid has provided in this paragraph the material item of study, its importance, and the central theme of her argument about mission gardens.

Let's look at an example of an introduction to a student paper, which combines the background with the central idea in one paragraph. We see similar organization in this text to the article we just examined. This is a paper that was written for the skyscraper assignment introduced earlier in the chapter.

1) Freemasonry, "having existed from time immemorial" has impacted and left a mark on places all over the world. 2) The marks made by the fraternity range from things on a grand scale such as new forms of government and society, to smaller things such as architecture. 3) Architecture, although a small thing within society, plays a pivotal role within the fraternity, for it is what the mason creates; as James Stevens Curl declares, it "[has] aspects capable of moving the beholder and an intellectual rigor." 4) There are many examples of Masonic architecture all over the country that get lots of attention, such as the Scottish Rite (an affiliated body to Freemasonry) Temple in Washington D.C.; however, there is an aspect of Masonic architecture that is not covered very well, and that is skyscrapers that were erected by the various lodges around the country. 5) There were quite a few magnificent skyscrapers built by the fraternity, and it is a mystery as to why they have not been focused on or discussed in depth. 6) Therefore, it is necessary to examine them and explain their different aspects, not only through obvious means such as the architectural details, but also by looking at and explaining some of the speculative parts of Freemasonry that would have influenced them.[3]

This student is building the background for his paper in much the same way Kryder-Reid did. He introduces a topic that is well known and relevant to the specific situation and the central point. In this case, sentences 1, 2, and 3 introduce us to the topic of Freemasonry and its relationship with architecture. Sentence 4) compares to sentence 1) of Kryder-Reid's in that it shows the gap in the literature—not much has been written about Freemason skyscrapers. Sentence 5) emphasizes the importance of the gap, so that the student can then in sentence 6) express the central idea of the paper, which contextualizes the approach the student will take in writing about the skyscrapers and their larger implications.

Note the importance in both examples of narrowing the focus of one's thesis statement. The same situation applies to arriving at a workable design concept. Often, you will find yourself initially with a general interest and only diffuse statements can be made as a result. This situation indicates that your understanding of the subject is still too introductory, too much on the surface. The thesis statement must be narrowed, usually as a result of further research, into a topic that can *both* provide direction for one's research as well as a right-sized topic for the length of one's assignment.

Notice in the first example that the topic is guided downward from California missions → mission landscapes → mission gardens and in the second example from Masonic buildings in general → Masonic skyscrapers. As it turns out, even this topic will be narrowed again into a collection of specific examples the author takes to be emblematic of the type. An architecture history survey course provides ample opportunity to pursue topics of interest and to develop interesting, focused thesis statements out of which a good paper can arise. Perhaps your interest is Gothic architecture. This is an enormous topic. See how you can begin to narrow it to the point that a workable, right-sized thesis statement can emerge. Gothic architecture → Gothic architecture in France → construction technology of French cathedrals → the evolution of the flying buttress in French cathedrals. Finally! Something of interest of sufficiently narrow scope that a thesis statement can be envisioned which can be argued for in the space allotted.

ANALYZING AND INCORPORATING EVIDENCE

After forming a thesis statement, the next logical task is usually to analyze your topic. Analyzing means that you break something complex into more easily understood parts. These parts may well include:

- Use of space
- Structure of buildings
- Movement or flow between or within buildings
- Function
- Artistic effects
- Materials

- Comparisons with surrounding environment or buildings
- Relationships with community, culture, tradition etc.
- Precedents
- Antecedents
- Place in the overall development of the type
- Intellectual history.

Analysis in writing history papers must include evidence. Evidence must be chosen to engage your claims and should be considered in light of the topic you are writing about and the claims you are making. Evidence supports the claims you are making; it is not the claim itself.

A good historian is a sleuth—combining as many different sources of evidence as possible in order to make the most coherent picture of what actually happened emerge. Historians make use of a large variety of evidentiary sources: archeological excavations, tax records, direct measurements, maps, photographs, geometric analysis, even graveyards and x-rays can be evidence. These are all possible (and interesting!) sources for your term paper, but the most readily available source of evidence in most cases is almost certainly what others have already written. This is why establishing, understanding, incorporating, and referring to the most authoritative texts on the subject takes on such importance.

When you are writing an analysis paper, you will want to present yourself as a credible, rational individual who uses architectural evidence to support the claims you are making. For that reason, you will want the focus of your writing to be on the topic itself, not on you as the writer. You will want to keep the reader's focus on the evidence and the analysis. That means you will want to break the evidence down in ways that help support the claim. You will also need to explain it to the reader. It is not always easy for the reader to understand why or how a piece of evidence relates to a claim, so you will have to make the connections explicit for your reader. You will also need to comment on the relevance of the evidence for your claim. Making the connections for the reader is of utmost importance for a successful paper. When we discuss paragraph development below, we illustrate how you can accomplish this in your paper.

MAKING AN ARGUMENT

Your assignment will typically ask you to make an argument about a building, a group of buildings, a particular architect's style or a period of architecture. Argument, in this case, means persuading your reader of an overall claim you are making. You take a particular position and proceed to try to convince your reader to adopt that stance, or at least think about the position you are claiming. Your analysis of the evidence will be the most important part of your writing for convincing your reader. Before you start writing, you should consider these factors, which will help you decide what claims and evidence will be most effective:

- *Purpose*: What is the purpose of this paper? For example, the purpose of the skyscraper paper is for the student to research some aspect of skyscrapers from a time period.
- *Audience*: Who will be reading this piece? What background knowledge does the reader have on the topic? What do you want the audience to learn from this or know that they didn't know before you started?

In the case of writing architectural history papers, your audience is generally your instructor, who can be expected to have good background knowledge of your topic. This may lead you to think that this person already knows the topic that you are going to write about, so you don't feel that you have much to add to his or her knowledge base. However, you need to take into consideration that he or she needs to be able to follow your organization and logic for your argument and may, in fact, learn something new in the process. And while there is probably little new regarding names and dates that a student can provide a history professor, there are always fresh interpretations or perceptions that you can uniquely apply to those names and dates. Thus, a student's task is twofold: to convince the reader that the student possesses adequate baseline knowledge, and to use that knowledge in the development of a unique voice.

Another aspect to consider when writing an argument paper is the importance of addressing counter-claims or opposing arguments. Your paper should reflect a consideration of counter-claims by either simply acknowledging them or by countering, minimizing, or proving them wrong. Your decision about how to engage the counter arguments should take into consideration your audience, your purpose, and the types of claims that you are making.

ORGANIZING AND DEVELOPING PARAGRAPHS

You will need to decide how to organize paragraphs in your paper. The organization should match the way you are approaching your topic. For example, if you are doing an overview of buildings over time or an architect's work over time, it makes sense to organize paragraphs by chronological elements. However, if covering a type of building spread geographically, you will need to decide how to organize your analysis spatially—you may want to ask whether there is a logic to ordering your analysis to particular examples. For example, the student who wrote the Freemason paper did so by discussing Masonic skyscrapers by city, alternating between Chicago, Minneapolis, and New York, and then finally to New Orleans. The reasons for shifting between cities had to do with the similarities in the buildings.

Oftentimes, paragraphs will act as organizers for your claims. For example, you could make your claim, provide evidence, and analyze the claim and evidence all in the same paragraph. That is to say, your analysis should show how your evidence relates to your claim because this will not always be self-evident to the reader.

See Kryder-Reid's paragraph below for an example of a strong paragraph that clearly makes its claim, provides evidence, and then ties the claim and evidence together.

1) As important as the production and dissemination of the Santa Barbara mission images are for understanding the site's place in American cultural memory, the nature of the reception of the images is equally significant, and it is useful to examine how these images were collected and consumed. 2) Personal

photograph albums from this period included both purchased photos and, with the advent of amateur photography, images taken by visitors to commemorate their own mission visits. 3) For example, Anthony Wayne Vodges, a career army officer, author, and fellow of the American Geological Society, created an album to record his California travels (1888–92) and selected nine photographs of the Santa Barbara Mission, including two views of the garden taken in 1888. 4) Private albums were both personal memory markers and mechanisms for sharing travels with friends and family. 5) The albums themselves became tangible spaces of memory and experience, capturing the mission visit at a specific moment and extending it through time, as the pages were turned, the images viewed, and stories told. 6) Postcards mailed or pasted in an album similarly concretized the visit with a visual memento that connected place, experience, and sentiment. 7) The images of the mission garden, whether it was perceived as shared heritage or as an exotic destination, fixed the public historic site as private memory.[4]

In sentence 1) the author provides a transition not only to a new paragraph but also to a new idea in the paper. She is shifting to how the images of the missions were received and what role that played in cultural memory. Remember that cultural memory is one of the larger claims of the paper itself. Sentence 2) then narrows to the focus of the particular paragraph, the personal photo albums— the evidence. Sentence 3) shows a particular example of the evidence by describing a particular individual's album. Sentences 4), 5), and 6) further provided evidence for the claim. Sentence 7) then ties the claim and the evidence back together. In this way, the paragraph ties together, in a convincing manner, the claim, the evidence and the analysis of the two.

INCLUDING VISUALS IN YOUR PAPER

You may be asked to include figures, drawings, or illustrations in your paper. Figures and illustrations are a specific kind of evidence that helps the reader see the connection you are making or clarify visually what you are describing in written form. Edward Tufte, author of the book *Beautiful Evidence,* says, "Evidence is evidence, whether words, numbers, images, diagrams, still or moving. The intellectual tasks remain constant regardless of the mode of evidence: to understand and to reason about the materials at hand, and to appraise their quality, relevance, and integrity."[5] He says that when you are presenting your evidence, you are engaging in analytical thinking: "understanding causality, making multi-variate comparisons, examining relevant evidence, and assessing the credibility of evidence and conclusions."[6] This means that you must do some decision-making about what visuals to include and how they might support your analysis or argument. Presenting visual evidence is also an ethical choice. You must consider how the visual is seen and consider its relevance and quality.

Always avoid providing free-floating images: referring to the visual in the text of the paper is necessary. One important point to remember is to place your reference in the text where it is relevant to what you are writing about and where the reader will find it most logical. In some cases, you will be asked to place the figure in the text; in others, you may be asked to put the figures in an appendix at the end of the text. In-text figures should be placed closely enough to the reference of the figure, so that it can help support the argument. Figures placed in an appendix should be identified as such for the reader to understand where to find them while reading. In addition, you should include a caption with the visual (Figure 3.2), which includes a title for the caption that is related to what you are writing about, and the credits for the visual (who was the originator of the photo or drawing).

As you decide on what figures to include in your text, you may want to ask yourself these questions:

- Does this figure support my text by
  - Showing comparisons, contrasts, differences?
  - Showing causality, or explanation or structure?
- Have I integrated words, images and numbers (if appropriate)?

FIGURE 3.2 The Modern Art Museum of Fort Worth, Texas (Tadao Ando, architect) demonstrates a highly refined technique with cast-in-place concrete

- Have I documented my figure? That is, provided a title, description, source information, or measurement scale?
- Does this figure match the content of my paper? That is, have I chosen a figure that shows quality, relevance and integrity in regard to the content of my paper? (Adapted from Tufte.)

DOCUMENTATION AND PLAGIARISM

Since writing architectural history is mainly an academic activity, relying on academic guidelines for credibility and ethics in terms of citing your sources is important. When you are writing an analysis or argument, you will be required to do research, and research requires documentation of sources. This involves more than not plagiarizing. This involves how the discourse community views conventions of citation for a particular field and the documentation style that supports that field. In architectural history, the *Chicago Manual of Style* is the standard. We will address some of the broader concerns having to do with citation, and then move to some more specific issues in the documenting of sources.

Plagiarism consists of taking someone else's language or ideas and claiming them as your own. This means that using someone else's sentence structure or even three words in a row from another source needs to be attributed to the author.

There are different levels of plagiarism, from outright intention to cheat, to unintended violations of citation practices. Many times, students are confused as to the conventions that dictate proper documentation of language and ideas.

There are ways you can avoid plagiarism:

- Start working on your paper early. Research takes time as does incorporating the research into your writing.
- When taking research notes, be sure to label the ideas and sentences that you have taken from the original source.

- When writing your paper, put your notes and source materials aside to prevent using the same language as the original sources.
- Make sure that you write down all the bibliographic information for each source and be sure to keep it with quotes, paraphrases, and summaries.
- If you have questions about how to cite or document a source, check with a style manual, your instructor or campus writing center.

Plagiarism is a serious offense, which could affect your college success or your career when you get into the workplace. If you have any questions about whether you are properly citing your sources, ask!

We have discussed the fact that writing never occurs in a vacuum; it is done within the context of a community of people whose practices inform the conventions of communication within that community. This goes for how texts interact with other texts, or what we might call "intertextuality." The fact is that, in order to demonstrate membership in an academic community, an individual must demonstrate his or her knowledge of the field. In addition, the individual must show familiarity with background knowledge of the particular topic he or she is working with, and be able to stand behind the evidence presented as support for claims. As a result, this means that other texts will be integrated with our texts. This requirement leads us to ask questions such as: What kinds of texts are appropriate? How many are enough? How does the information get integrated with my text?

We have addressed the first question, 'What kinds of texts are appropriate?' in the first part of the chapter when discussing evidence. The texts that you include in history papers should be considered evidence (they do not stand in for your claims). They should be appropriate for the type of analysis you are doing. We emphasized the importance of this for figures as well.

In terms of the second question—often the number of sources will be determined by your instructor. If that information is not made clear, and you are confused, you may want to ask the instructor how many sources might be appropriate for the length and type of paper you are writing. In addition, you will want to survey the literature on your topic to see what has been done in the area you are studying. See what sources relate directly to your topic and the scope of your topic. Then, as you are writing your paper, determine which sources might support your claims most effectively.

We will spend the most time here with the third question: How does the information get integrated with my text?

First, you will want to think about how to package the information. Do you want to express it as a paraphrase, summary or quotation? A paraphrase takes a small part of a text or an idea and puts it into your words. A summary is a more extensively structured piece in which you put the text into your own words, and a quotation consists of the exact words of the source author. Most of the time you will not be summarizing a long text, so we will focus on paraphrase and quotation here. Having said that, the rule of thumb is to paraphrase more than quote. Quoting should be reserved for times when the original source author has said something in such a unique way that it is difficult to summarize. Quoting may include quoting a full sentence or part of a sentence from the source author. If we look to our mission gardens example, Table 3.1 shows that of the 109 notes in the article the majority of the types of source citation come in the form of the paraphrase.

TABLE 3.1

Type of citation	Number	Percentage
Paraphrase	73	67%
Notes	10	9%
Quotes (full sentence)	10	9%
Quotes (integrated with sentences)	10	9%
Quotes (around a word or phrase in a sentence)	6	6%
Total	**109**	**100%**

Notes that were not connected with a particular source made up 9 percent of the total number of notes. That is, they were acknowledgments or background information. In addition, we can see that quotes total 24 percent of the total. However, most of those quotes were integrated into sentences such as "The neophyte residences were vacant shells, the corrals empty, and 'the palm trees are dead, and the olive and fig trees are dilapidated and broken'." Or, the quotation marks were integrated with just a word or phrase quoted from the original: "The fountain scene, with its interplay of light and shadow, patina and palm, its erasure of the Native American past, and its capture of the quintessential mission architectural forms has become what MacCannell has called 'constructed recognition'."[7] Many of the quotes, whether full sentences or integrations into sentences were descriptions from first-hand experience:

> In the same essay, however, Saunders wistfully imagined that "in sunny corners and against sheltering walls the padres would plant their roses of Castille and lilies of Mary, their hollyhocks and malvarosas, their oleanders and many another dear flower of that far-off Mediterranean home which most of them were destined never to see again".[8]

Never leave quotes unanchored to drift about in your paragraphs. They should always be integrated into a sentence or preceded by an introductory phrase.

Another decision to make is whether to include the author's name as part of the paraphrase. When you are quoting it is a good idea to always include the author's name in the introductory phrase to the quote. In addition, *Chicago* style asks that you include the full name of the author on first mention and then the last name thereafter. When you are paraphrasing, you will need to decide whether you want to bring the readers' attention to the information or to the person who presented the information. Again, this information will depend on your topic and how you approach it. If you are analyzing a building (or set of buildings) or a style of a time period, you may want to keep the information prominent and just include the number or the author's name and date parenthetically at the end of the sentence or paragraph. If comparing scholars' or architects' views or positions or highlighting a person who may have coined a term or presented a new idea, you will want to include the source author's name when introducing the paraphrase.

The first sentence of the mission garden article starts with an author prominent quote:

> In his book *The Old Franciscan Missions of California*, George Wharton James, a prolific chronicler of the California missions, wrote: "The story of the Old Missions of California is perennially new. The interest in the ancient and dilapidated buildings and their history increases with each year. To-day a thousand visit them where ten saw them twenty years ago, and twenty years hence, hundreds of thousands will stand in their sacred precincts, and unconsciously absorb beautiful and unselfish lessons of life as they hear some part of their history recited."[9]

In this case, in addition to the author's name, the title of the book AND a bit of biographical information is included. In history papers, this strategy should be used less than introducing the author's last name.

When paraphrasing, use author-prominent introductions less than information-prominent.

- Author prominent: "The scholarship of W.J.T. Mitchell, John Dixon Hunt, and other theorists and landscape historians inspires an exploration of the hermeneutics of the mission landscapes—how they were known and understood over time and how they have become woven into the tapestry of California memory."[10]
- Information prominent: "This conflation of colonial mission and garden maintains an enduring influence on California cultural memory."[11]

Chicago style allows both the author/date system of documentation and the notes system of documentation. In both the student paper and the journal article we have been using as examples, the notes system has been used. This means that each citation is numbered sequentially with superscript numbers throughout the paper and the list of numbers with the bibliographic information is contained at the bottom of the page in a footnote or at the end of the paper in endnotes. Be sure to place your numbers at the end of a sentence (not in the middle) and after all punctuation marks.

The author/date system of documentation requires that the author's last name and the date (year) of the source are placed in the text at the appropriate place (after quote or paraphrase) and the bibliographic information is placed at the end of the paper with the title "Bibliography" or "Works Cited." The Bibliography is arranged alphabetically by last name of the author. This system may be somewhat easier for the author than is the notes system, but has the disadvantage of interrupting the flow of the argument for the reader.

Be sure that your in-text citations and your notes or bibliography match. That is, be sure that whatever you have cited in your paper appears in your footnotes, endnotes or on your Bibliography page.

SETTING UP A QUOTE OR ATTRIBUTION

One of the most difficult aspects of quoting and paraphrasing is smoothly integrating the attribution with the material. That is, how to introduce the quote or paraphrase into your text without using awkward means to do so. The material that precedes a quote or a paraphrase is often called a "signal phrase" or an "introductory phrase." In *Chicago* style, use the present tense or present perfect in introductory phrases, but unless there is good reason to emphasize that something was said in the past, do not use past tense.

Here are some helpful verbs to use in introductory phrases: *agrees, points out, declares, reports, suggests, claims, asserts, emphasizes, denies* (among others).

Present tense use of verb *claim*:

Meredith Clausen claims that unlike other areas of architectural history, the Ecole des Beaux-Arts did have women, "The same could be said of the Ecole des Beaux-Arts, with one major difference: women *were* there, their presence in history overlooked, ignored, or relegated to a parenthetical footnote or paragraph, and left wholly out of the main discourse."[12]

Present perfect use of phrasal verb *pointed out*:

Charles Anthony Stewart has pointed out that by "recognizing these common factors perhaps historians can be less rigid as they differentiate between Eastern and Western architecture development."[13]

Notice that the present tense example with an introductory phrase used a comma before the quotations marks. In the second, the quotation is integrated into the sentence grammatically. When integrating a quote into a sentence, be sure the grammar matches the sentence grammar.

In terms of punctuating introductory phrases, the most common form of punctuation is the comma. However, if you are using a formal introductory phrase using *thus*, or *as follows*, you will want to use a colon. A period is used when introducing a block quote.[14]

Difficulty in Setting up a Quote or Attribution

Consider, first, this cumbersome way of informing the reader what a lecturer said.

During Dr. Michael Braungart's lecture on his book, *Cradle to Cradle*, he said that the first step toward sustainability is redesigning the relationship between industry and nature.

Not only is it cumbersome, but it is also unclear where the author's language leaves off and the lecturer's begins. Three changes are needed. First, let the pronoun "his" come before the lecturer's name in the sentence. This approach allows the lecturer's proper name to be the high point of the sentence as well as provide a lead into the quote. Second, identify the quoted material. Finally, the word "during" imparts the sense that this quote was out of the mainstream of the lecture. That is to say, that something happened during the lecture that interrupted it. So let's change that word:

> In his lecture on his book *Cradle to Cradle*, Dr. Michael Braungart said that the first step toward sustainability is "redesigning the relationship between industry and nature."

Now consider this attribution of another writer's ideas:

> In Barbara Nadel's essay, "Listening to Engineers," she outlines the architect/engineer relationship.

The set-up of this attribution can be greatly simplified by eliminating the pronoun "she" altogether:

> Barbara Nadel's essay "Listening to Engineers" outlines the architect/engineer relationship.

Try reading the following passage aloud:

> Robert Ivy, editor of Architectural Record, wrote saying, "Architecture for Humanity represents the finest. . ."

The phrase "wrote saying" becomes obviously redundant. Eliminate the word "saying" and the sentence reads perfectly well.

The problem with the following set-up of a quote is the careless employ of the preposition "with" which then turns the rightful subject of the sentence, Rem Koolhaas, into a prepositional phrase requiring the further addition of the pronoun "he."

> In an interview with Rem Koolhaas he stated that "it is a hopeless battle to change. . ."

Eliminate the word "with" and the pronoun "he" can disappear as well:

> In an interview Rem Koolhaas stated that "it is a hopeless battle to change . . ."

LANGUAGE CONVENTIONS

We take the view in this book that language doesn't just refer to ideas and concepts, but that it also creates social relations. In the case of writing, this means how the writers position themselves in order to connect with the reader. A discourse community has its conventions for the types of language it uses—this includes not just the obvious specialized vocabulary choices but also sentence structure and language choices that send messages about the writer's position toward the information that he/she is writing about.

In general, you will want to use complex sentence structure for analysis and argument. Writing the history paper also means using a more formal academic tone and complex sentences. However, it is often effective to vary the sentence structure in a paragraph to give the reader a rhythm and to show the flow of the information. For example this paragraph from the mission garden article makes its claim with a simple sentence. It then moves to its evidence with a complex sentence and analyzes with the use of a compound sentence.

> *Simple*:
> The mission garden was an invention of the late nineteenth century.[15]

> *Complex*:
> From the initial vision and intent of the creators who planted ornamental gardens in formerly utilitarian courtyards, beginning

with Father José Maria Romo at the Santa Barbara Mission in 1872, the social meanings of mission gardens have been constituted by the performance of the space by those who lived, worked, and visited them, including the resident Franciscans, visiting dignitaries, pilgrims, parishioners, artists, and tourists.[16]

Compound:
These meanings have been made tangible and communicated to a broader audience through text, image, and other material culture, and these representations have codified the constructed image of the sites as historic relics and beautiful, sacred spaces.[17]

You will also want to take into consideration your use of transitions between ideas as well as being aware of how you are signaling your information to the reader.

Transitions include such words as a*dditionally, again, also, although, as a result, besides, but, consequently, conversely, equally, further, hence, however, in contrast, likewise, moreover, rather, so, therefore, thus, while*, etc.

These words, used effectively, can help give the reader insight into where you are leading him or her. Let's look at a sentence presented earlier:

While the history of the mission buildings is relatively well documented, the associated landscapes have received much less scrutiny.[18]

The transition word *while* tells the reader that the writer is conceding that something is the case in the subordinate clause (underlined), so the expectation is that there will be a contrast or claim made in the main clause that will be important for what follows. In fact, this transition sentence, which occurs at the beginning of the paragraph, is very important in helping the author build to the thesis or main claim or focus of the article.

There are other kinds of markers that help you guide your reader through the text such as markers that help with:[19]

- Sequencing information: *first, last, subsequently, then, to begin*, etc.
- Label progressions: *all in all, at this point, in conclusion, thus far, therefore, overall, to summarize*.
- Announce your goals for various parts of the paper: *aim, focus, goal, objective, purpose, want to, intend to*.
- Shift topics: *now, move on, well, turn to, back to, so, with regard to*.

There are also ways to show your attitude toward an idea that you have written: *admittedly, appropriate, correctly, desirable, essential, disappointingly, interestingly, surprised, unexpected*.

Or you may want to establish the certainty with which you regard the information: *actually, always, certain, decidedly, evidently, in fact, indeed, indisputable, known, thinks, undeniable, true, obviously, surely, of course*.

When you balance these certainty words with qualifiers such as *seem, usually, may, fairly, almost, appears, claims, estimated, generally, guess, indicate, in most cases, in my opinion, perhaps, presumably* you can establish a kind of credibility with your reader that shows your confidence with the information without overstating your position.

When writing on academic topics and working to paraphrase into your own language, or trying to write a difficult idea, you may find that your sentences contain faulty predication or subject-verb agreement problems. Faulty predication is a term that is used when the noun in a sentence cannot do what the verb it is paired with is asking it to do. Let's look at an example.

The purpose of concrete was invented to provide stable foundations for buildings.

Purpose cannot be invented. See the following correct sentence:

Concrete was invented to provide stable foundations for buildings.

Be sure that your verbs are paired with nouns that can do the action of the verb.

Subject-verb problems often come when there is an intervening prepositional phrase between the noun and the verb. For example:

One of the porticos are hidden from sight by a grove of trees.

In this case, "one" is the subject of the sentence, but the writer has made the verb agree with the object of the prepositional phrase, "porticos." To remedy this make the verb agree with "one":

One of the porticos is hidden from sight by a grove of trees.

There are other grammatical issues that may arise as you are working on your history paper, but these are some that we find are common among students.

USING ARCHITECTURAL TERMS ACCURATELY

Every part of a building has a name. Possessing adequate subject matter knowledge to write effectively includes knowing the proper architectural terminology for the elements you are describing or at least having a good reference at hand to help. Even if it were not beyond the scope of this book to provide a dictionary of architectural terms, it would not be necessary because a number of architectural dictionaries already exist. We suggest you have one at your side as you begin your career as a writer. Henry Parker's *Concise Dictionary of Architectural Terms* is one such resource. Cyril M. Harris' *Dictionary of Architecture and Construction* is remarkably thorough but may be less useful if you are searching for a particular name of an architectural element based on its use. Francis Ching's *A Visual Dictionary of Architecture* groups elements into themes which, combined with numerous line drawings, may be more help in this regard. Ernest Burden's *Illustrated Dictionary of Architecture* also does some grouping and leans toward photographic illustration of terms. Fleming, Honour and Pevsner's *Penguin Dictionary of Architecture and Landscape Architecture* runs strictly alphabetically but often includes considerable background information. James Stevens Curl's *Oxford Dictionary of Architecture and Landscape Architecture* is a similar entrant.

WRITING A CONCLUSION

Writing conclusions is often a perplexing process when you are new to writing in this genre. Introductions and conclusions frame the paper with the main thrust of our argument, the "so what" of the paper. In the introduction, we meet the reader at common ground, attract attention to the topic, and then move from there logically to the main point of the paper. The conclusion works this process in reverse: we have led the reader through our argument and now we want to tie back to the original main point and then gently move back out to how our main point connects with the common ground. However, because the reader and writer have traversed the argument through the paper, the reader is not in the same place as where she started, so a simple restatement of the main idea is not enough. The "so what" of the paper needs to be reinforced using the reader's newly acquired knowledge. That means that now your main idea is reinforced by the points that you have made and the implications of what you have argued in the paper. You may now make connections to broader issues, challenge the reader, point the reader to the future, or pose a question. Since the conclusion is the final word, it needs to be powerful enough that the reader will remember the main message of the paper.

The introductory and final paragraphs of the mission gardens article are included here to illustrate how beginnings and endings frame the historical research. These do not fully represent the introduction and conclusion of the article—both are much longer. However, for your own paper, you will probably be able to contain your introductions and conclusions in a paragraph or two. See the following introductory paragraph:

> In his book *The Old Franciscan Missions of California*, George Wharton James, a prolific chronicler of the California missions, wrote: "The story of the Old Missions of California is perennially new. The interest in the ancient and dilapidated buildings and their history increases with each year. To-day a thousand visit them where ten saw them twenty years ago, and twenty years hence, hundreds of thousands will stand in their sacred precincts, and unconsciously absorb beautiful and unselfish lessons of life as they hear some part of their history recited." Writing almost a century ago, James made several prescient observations about the mission landscapes, for just as he predicted, the missions have been "perennially new" because each generation has shaped the spaces and inscribed on them their notions of the past. They have been reinvented by their organic, evolving principles of design and by their changing reception. As much as the mission landscapes have changed over the past two centuries, however, they remain remarkably indelible symbols of a venerable and venerated heritage. James recognized the importance of the sites for informing the public's notion of the past as they "unconsciously absorb . . . their history recited," and his allusion to "beautiful and unselfish lessons" underscores their enduring ideological and political meanings.[20]

Kryder-Reid sets up the theme of missions (which she then narrows to mission gardens in paragraph three, which we saw earlier in the chapter), and their historical political, and symbolic importance in the first paragraph. Interest is created through the use of a quote. Now take a look at the concluding paragraph:

> While the politics of race and power have been and continue to be inscribed in the mission gardens, their popularity also offers an intellectually accessible and physically tangible opportunity for spurring dialogue about the historiography of the sites. The gardens offer an opportunity to expand the

concept of historic preservation to include cultural landscapes. While a number of the missions are on the National Register, none lists the gardens as contributing resources, despite the fact that they are some of the oldest gardens in the state. Caring for the gardens is generally the responsibility of volunteers or the general maintenance staff, or the work is contracted out to landscaping companies with little or no consideration of the historic plant material or the multivalent histories of the spaces. By developing stewardship programs that address the historic significance of the gardens and interpretive programs that reveal the social relationships and ideologies encoded in the landscapes, the sites have the potential to become a locus for dialogue about the history of the missions and allow us to reexamine accepted notions of California history.[21]

In the conclusion, the themes introduced at the beginning of the article are restated, but there is also a call for change—that the landscapes and gardens be included as part of the historical record and that they be recognized for their political and ideological contributions.

When you are writing a conclusion, you may want to think about using some of the following strategies to leave a mark on the mind of your reader:

- Place a strategic quotation
- Create a call to action
- Evoke an image
- Suggest an implication
- Discuss how your findings relate to a broader topic

Remember that introductions and conclusions are the readers' first and last impression of your work and will have the largest impact.

The genre of writing history in architecture is an important one for you as a student. This type of writing will help you develop an understanding of the field of architecture and its cultural, political, and historical context. To steep yourself in this context by writing about an era, type of building, architect, or style of architecture means that you are placing yourself in professional shoes, so to speak, in which you will be able to walk forward into the other design challenges that await you in your curriculum.

exercises

1. Read the following quote and paraphrase it. Include an effective introduction to the paraphrase.

   Recent scholarship has illuminated the formal heterogeneity of the modernisms of the 1950s, but although Byrne and Iannelli had practiced such heterogeneity since 1914 and would pursue it until 1964, their contribution to the diversity of early modernism remains underappreciated.[22]

2. Go through a draft of your history paper and check to see whether you have varied your sentence structure. How many simple, compound, complex or compound-complex sentences do you have in your paper?

3. Choose a paragraph in your paper and check your use of transitions. Have you used the transitions appropriately? Do they convey confidence in your argument?

PROJECT DESCRIPTIONS

Why is it necessary to write about your work, your project, your design, when you can just show it and stand back? Writing about one's work is indispensable for several reasons. Though the visual is a speedy, powerful medium for conveying information, it can often be overwhelming. Writing helps call attention to *what about* the project is most significant. Images and models, unless you make many of them as you go, are insufficient for explaining the designer's thought process. For this you need words, words organized into sentences that build upon one another to explain *why* the project resulted in *this particular set* of images and models and not one of the infinite possible alternatives. Finally, of course, you must consider the fundamental reason behind the practice of making presentations: it is to arrive at a mutual understanding between presenter and audience. Since humans are fundamentally language-driven beings, language is how we come to agreement. Images, gestures and grunts will never be adequate substitutes. To develop an overall sense of the process of refining a description of one's work before analyzing the genre in more detail, let's jump right in with revising this paraphrased description of a remodeled urban penthouse flat that is in much need of revision (Figure 4.1). In addition to some easily corrected grammatical problems, it suffers from more basic problems of logic, flow, and tone and it fails to give justice to the elegance of the design work:

Fantastic skyline views. A narrow gallery connecting the living pavilions places circulation along the north wall. Solar gain is provided by south facing glass.

Natural wood cabinetry defines the circulation path negotiating between framed and expansive views. Openings between the internal/external spaces allow for entertaining through the full length of the house and enjoying natural daylighting.

There is no need for decoration—just openness to the outdoors.

Though the grammatical problems may be the first thing to jump out, it would be a mistake to begin by correcting these elements when the basic structure is in so much need of work. The author has fundamentally failed to recognize that an adequate description of one's project requires a sense of order and of

FIGURE 4.1 "Fantastic Skyline Views"

progression every bit as much as does a history term paper. In place of discussing the reasoning behind the design, the author has provided what nearly reads as a bulleted list of features—something that might be acceptable in a real estate advertisement but is not when discussing the product of one's intellectual efforts. Designers must be on guard against succumbing to the real estate developer's amenity-driven mentality when discussing their work. A work of architecture doesn't result from the piling on of features no matter how glamorous. Even if "three bedrooms, 2½ baths, granite kitchen counters, great views, and a hot tub" are all true, they do not, in themselves, ever add up to a work of architecture because a work of architecture is fundamentally idea-driven—and hot tubs are not ideas. So the description must be organized so that the features follow naturally from the basic premise on which the building was conceived. Herein lies the first task: the description is in need of a design premise. The description has provided little guidance to understanding what drove the designer's thinking toward realizing this particular design.

Clues to what it might be, however, do present themselves. The opener, "Fantastic skyline views," even though a sentence fragment and hence undecipherable for meaning, is probably an important generating influence given the generally positive connotation of the word "fantastic" and the fragment's placement at the beginning of the discussion. Furthermore, context usually is significant (and at the least should never go unmentioned). Indeed, openness to the views is discussed a second time, so this is probably a good assumption. So, capitalizing on the beautiful views offered by the flat's location will be assumed a prime design generator, but this cannot be the whole story because it fails to account for division of the flat into two pavilions. Spatial organization is basic to any architectural design task, so it must invariably be accounted for in the premise. In this case, the division corresponds to organizing the more public spaces together and the more private sleeping and study spaces together. The relatively public spaces, unsurprisingly, have more glass and a greater sense of expansion to the outdoors than do the private spaces. With this much in mind—a contextual response is combined with a basic internal organization—the revised description can at least be begun.

The owner wished for a living area maximally open to the south-facing city views combined with a stronger sense of enclosure for the sleeping rooms. This led to a two-pavilion scheme whereby the nearly all-glass living spaces are separated from the more private spaces by a thin, cabinetry-lined corridor.

Now the division of the building into two distinct parts makes sense as a logical expression of a concise idea about how the owner wished to live in her home; before, not only did the idea of distinct pavilions seem at least potentially arbitrary, but also vague as to just how many pavilions the building actually consisted.

Now understanding that the building consists of two distinct parts, the reader, to gain a better mental picture, will naturally want to know more about them—how they are organized and how they differ. This is where the part of the original description, the sentence about "the internal/external spaces," probably does more to confuse than to enlighten. First of all, the use of the word "the" in front of internal/external presumes that the subject has already been discussed. For example, if I were describing the appliances in a kitchen as consisting of "a dishwasher, Sub-Zero refrigerator and a down-draft range," then I could move on to a fuller discussion of features of "the range" and the reader would intuitively grasp that this was the same range mentioned earlier and not another range elsewhere in the house. But this simple strategy is not employed here. Using the word "the" in this instance makes the reader wonder if he has missed the introduction of the subject in an earlier sentence—hence confusion, not clarity, is the result. But misuse of the article "the" isn't the worst of it. Use of slash marks in sentences is almost always to be avoided. It eviscerates meaning. In rare occasions, such as when referring to an "on/off switch" or a "yes/no vote," one wishes to indicate the existence of only two mutually exclusive states of affairs. *Then* a slash may be in order. But what the author here wishes to do is almost the exact opposite. Rather than refer to a mutually exclusive state of affairs, the author wishes to indicate the lengths the designer went to elide the distinction between indoors and out, but this is no way to do it.

Finally, in the same sentence, the phrase "and enjoying natural daylighting" is a faulty predication. Are the spaces themselves "enjoying natural daylighting"? Does it even make sense that a space would "enjoy"? Yet, that is the only subject in the sentence for the phrase to refer. Of course it should be "the owners" or "owners and guests" or "occupants" or other sentient beings that do the enjoying. Thus, this sentence as it stands is pretty catastrophic. To work, it will need an entirely new introductory sentence explaining how the designer combines indoors and outdoors and it will need to rework the tacked-on phrase concerning the abundant daylighting.

> The more public pavilion combines kitchen, dining and living areas into one large space, which opens onto flanking outdoor living areas through sliding glass walls. For large parties these walls remain open to expand the available space, blur the division between indoors and out, and provide abundant natural light. The more private pavilion has internal partitions separating sleeping rooms and bathrooms and provides smaller, framed openings to city views.

This last sentence performs two tasks: it describes what makes the bedroom wing more private, and it improves on the vague phrase from the earlier sentence "negotiating between framed and expansive views," by stating where the expansive views can be obtained (the public pavilion) and where the framed views are to be found. Furthermore, it overcomes the lack of referent for the phrase "framed view." Framed view of what? As it stood, the author just assumed that the framed view was also of the city, but it could have just as easily been of a drainpipe or fire escape. Greater specificity was needed.

The problems with the final sentence, "There is no need for decoration—just openness to the outdoors," are primarily grammatical. It actually does a respectable job of providing a rationale for the minimalist detailing and lack of molding in the building by referring back to the premise that the view is driving the design decisions and therefore the designer wants to avoid elements that will call attention to themselves. This takes the description down to the level of fine detail as well as ties it back to the concept. What is problematic is that it is both wordy and jagged. The phrase "There is" is almost always to be avoided. The subject of the sentence shouldn't be an existential "there" but rather the lack of decoration. Thus, leaving off "there is" altogether and beginning with "No need for decoration" gets right to the real subject. But the predicate phrase "just openness" is slangy and too informal for the objective tone of the rest of the description. "No need for decoration—just openness to the outdoors" is now no longer a sentence once the dreadful "there is" is eliminated.

> Detailing is minimalist—no need for distracting decoration when the views provide such an arresting backdrop.

Now we are in position to put the description back together.

> The owner wished for a living area maximally open to the south-facing city views combined with a stronger sense of enclosure for the sleeping rooms. This led to a two-pavilion scheme whereby the nearly all-glass living spaces are separated from the more private spaces by a thin cabinetry-lined corridor. The more public pavilion combines kitchen, dining and living areas into one large space, which opens onto flanking outdoor living areas through sliding glass walls. For large parties these walls remain open to expand the available space, blur the distinction between indoors and out, and provide abundant natural light. The more private pavilion has internal partitions separating sleeping rooms and bathrooms and provides smaller, framed openings to city views. Detailing is minimalist—no need for distracting decoration when the views provide such an arresting backdrop.

Note the cumulative improvements: what was a list of unordered items now has a logic to its presentation and a beginning, middle, and end. It flows from the broadest ideas to the most specific. The design rationale is manifest in each sentence. Words are used economically to consistently maintain an objective tone. It starts with that all-important design premise.

THE PREMISE—THE BEGINNING

The premise gives the designer something to test ideas against
and the reader the means to judge the degree to which the
designer succeeded according to her own criteria. In the description
above, the premise concerned accommodating distinctly public and
private needs within the same building while respecting an open
orientation to an urban context. A reading of the context is
oftentimes the jumping-off point, as it is for the following
design premise:

> The site occupies a transition point between industrial and
> commercial buildings to the east and residential buildings to
> the west. Much of the design is driven by our desire to
> finesse that transition.

Reading a premise like this, certain expectations of
the design in terms of forms, materials, and scale already begin
to present themselves. How well the designer addresses these
expectations will determine whether the reader is persuaded that
the design makes sense. Thus, a good premise or concept
becomes a yardstick against which to measure the designer's
success given her own goals. Beware ostensible concepts or
premises that are too

- Abstract: "The concept of this building is motion."
  Since few buildings have large-scale moving parts, the
  word "motion" is unlikely to have any direct bearing on
  architectural concerns. So as it stands, the word
  could mean too many things to base a design premise
  on it.
- Metaphorical: "The design is based upon the opening
  of a flower." Invoking the metaphor of an opening flower
  might well serve to help develop imagery and form, but
  lacks a rationale. "*Why* a flower?" a reader might reasonably
  ask.
- Vague: "This building is about the human body in space."
  But what *about* the body in space?

- Laudable but over-ambitious: "The concept of this building is to knit the community together." Few building occasions are momentous enough to hold up under such weighty expectations. If the building serves its occupants well but doesn't quite measure up to healing an urban fabric, must it then be considered a failure?
- Egocentric: "I wanted this building to reveal itself in layers." What do you suppose the occupants wanted?
- Negative: "I didn't think the building should meekly blend-in." Design is a goal-driven activity. To seek to *not* do something can seldom be termed a "goal."

While the above have in common a certain overwhelming grandeur, the same problem results from excessively modest aspirations as well:

> We wanted to create a LEED-certified (or BREEAM-certified) home. *Achieving certification for a high-level of sustainability is certainly to be congratulated. But so many ways to do this exist that it fails to provide enough of a rationale to determine the major design decisions.*

> The client desired an up-to-date office building and pleasant work environment. *"Up-to-date" depends too significantly on one's temporal reference point to be of much use by itself while "pleasant" is simply too subjective a term against which to measure design decisions.*

Aside from the ho-hum quality of these two statements, they simply permit too much to be sufficiently action-guiding. An equally debilitating problem comes from premises that are too narrowly defined:

> I wanted the design to address the southeast corner. *This is fine as far as it goes, but one wonders what thought will go into determining the arrangement of spaces and the form of the other three-fourths of the building.*

This building is about the light-transmitting qualities of glass block. *The problem here is that the task of exploiting the properties of a single material almost certainly operates at a higher level of specificity than is needed for such fundamental design tasks as organizing the functional spaces.*

While these statements at least impart a few expectations against which to measure the success or failure of the design, the problem is that they seek to elevate a feature into a premise making it impossible for the premise to take on the task of providing guidance for a majority of the design decisions. Both statements call forth a too-detailed level of specificity to be design generators. Thus, writing a successful premise is to a considerable degree a question of achieving a proper scope: it must have a loose fit—neither so blanketing that anything goes, nor so snug that space for possible decisions is artificially constrained.

A design premise emanating from a critical attitude toward what came before or what is nearby may well be adequate to drive the major design decisions. For instance, for two of the newer colleges of Cambridge University that sit opposite one another, Clare Hall and Robinson College, it could be said that their design concepts present contrasting ideas of how the modern residential college should be organized. The 1960s-era design of Clare Hall seeks to breakdown the traditional formality of the medieval-based college by creating an academic village distinctly lacking in signs of hierarchy. It has multiple entries; its scale is distinctly residential; its form is broken into discreet, separate buildings. The later Robinson College seeks to reinstate or preserve some of the formality and grandeur that once placed college life outside the hustle of daily life with a modern interpretation of a medieval castle precinct. It has a single entry recalling a drawbridge and portcullis; it is one of the tallest buildings among the colleges, and all the diverse functional elements are housed in what appears to be a single, L-shaped block (Figure 4.2). Thus, in both cases, immediate design implications follow from the premise. One would expect Robinson to be large, imposing, enclosing a significant amount of outdoor space, and largely of one material. From Clare's premise, in contrast, one would

a)   b)

FIGURE 4.2 Clare Hall and Robinson College, Cambridge University, entrances

expect relatively intimately scaled surroundings, a distinct disregard for a strong formal hierarchy, and a diverse materials palette. In both cases, one's expectations would not be disappointed. Such is the power of a well-conceived premise.

For some designers, a premise is an expression of an ongoing interest they have, be it pushing the sustainability agenda, rebuilding poverty-torn communities, or exploring the possibilities of computer-generated form, to name but three. Designs will follow from these ongoing investigations, building upon lessons learned from previous outings. Thus, the same premise may apply to several projects. This is the case for the Greenbridge project in North Carolina by the notable sustainable design firm of William McDonough + Partners:

> Envisioned by our client as a model for conscious living, Greenbridge offers a positive strategy for suburban areas by demonstrating smart growth principles in action.[1]

Keep in mind, this premise is not simply an empty marketing ploy with feel-good phrases, but uses a key term—suburban smart growth principles—that should provide the project with an action-guiding design concept. Note that this premise doesn't give the specifics of the context or even mention the building type because it doesn't really have to; a certain generic type of site and a mixture of uses is implied by the key term.

The injunction that a premise should not be too abstract does not mean that it cannot be an expression of highly theoretical interests. However, highly theoretical interests are no excuse for vagueness. For example, Peter Eisenman writes of a highly theory-laden idea turned into a recognizable premise:

> Suppose for a moment that architecture could be conceptualized as a Moebius strip, with an unbroken continuity between interior and exterior. What would this mean for vision? Gilles Deleuze has proposed just such a possible continuity with his idea of the fold. For Deleuze, folded space articulates a new relationship between vertical and horizontal, figure and ground, inside and out—all structures articulated by traditional vision . . . My folded projects are a primitive beginning. In them the subject understands that he or she can no longer conceptualise experience in space in the same way that he or she did in gridded space.[2]

From this, of necessity more lengthy premise, a certain design approach with recognizable and verifiable results can begin to be envisioned.

Many buildings out in the world have no real premise to their design, or else the premise is so commonplace that it hardly bears mentioning. Think, for example, of the two-story motels littering the highways. They have no real design premise (they may have other premises-financial premises, for example). However, this should never be the case in a project during school. A major objective of a design education is to help students recognize and act on worthwhile premises. Once this hurdle is cleared, explaining the project itself in terms of the premise follows naturally.

Project Description—The Body

When explaining the design that follows from the premise, one will never be able to say everything that could be said about the project without reader fatigue, tedium, or outright boredom. Judicious editing is required to select the most important features—those that illustrate the premise. The explanation of the project following the premise should illustrate or substantiate that the stated concept was indeed the guiding idea.

Here's how William McDonough + Partners describes the Greenbridge project in such a way as to substantiate the premise of suburban smart growth:

> Through a series of terraces and a large central courtyard, sunlight penetrates all public areas, offices and apartments. The design optimizes energy use, comfort, individual control, feedback and adaptability. Roof surfaces will be productive— used to grow plants and food, generate power, and provide places to play and rest.[3]

Note that this description sensibly moves from overall massing "terraces . . . central courtyard" to more specific sustainability strategies in the second sentence, to an individual feature—the roof—in the third. Furthermore, the discussion of the roof isn't just *another* feature, it is an aspect of the design that gives concrete realization to the strategies outlined in the second sentence. In this way, the description also becomes a tightly woven argument for the building.

Similarly, Peter Eisenman for his Wexner Center for the Visual Arts, illustrates how his theory-conscious premise is turned into a work of architecture:

> The Center can be described as a non-building—an archaeological earthwork whose essential elements are scaffolding and landscaping. The scaffolding consists of two intersecting three-dimensional gridded corridors which link the existing performance hall and auditorium with the new

galleries and arts facilities being constructed. One arm of the scaffolding is aligned with the campus grid, the other scaffolding is aligned with the City of Columbus street grid which is 12-1/2 degrees askew. Hence, the project both physically and symbolically links the campus and the city beyond. But it does not do so in a holistic, unifying way because the building itself is fractured and incomplete looking.[4]

Note that while Eisenman does include some functional aspects to his description, they are carefully crafted to support his design thinking. The two concluding sentences are built from the descriptions that preceded them. While this description does not eschew all practicality, note that discussion of such ordinarily relevant information as what functions the building actually houses is resisted; relegated, according to his premise, to the level of mere pretext to engage in the type of design thinking that really engages his creative impulse. But even so, the description conforms to the basic format of moving from the general to the specific. First we are told that overall form has two "essential elements." Then one of the elements—the scaffolding—is discussed in greater detail in the next two sentences to justify the assertion in the fourth sentence that the project links the campus with the city. The fifth sentence describes the overall aesthetic effect he believes he has achieved. This highly intellectually challenging exercise of incorporating a design theory into a work of architecture is no excuse for muddled writing. If anything, it demands even greater clarity and a stronger sense of organization than do more conventional design statements. Though striving to exceed one's current design capabilities is always praiseworthy, if the result is an inability to clearly communicate the design intent or the resulting project, then there is no choice but to drop back to more familiar themes that *can* be communicated clearly. The chances of creating a project that isn't at least as muddled as what one is able to say about it are poor indeed. Design clarity depends on one's ability to articulate that design. If you cannot write or speak clearly about your design project, it is highly unlikely that you are thinking clearly about it.

Thus, virtually any description of one's work, whether of a pragmatic of theoretical stripe, will be governed by the same conventions: it proceeds from the general to the specific, from the overall massing to the most significant elements which substantiate that the premise was indeed put into action.

THE SUMMATION SENTENCE

Achieving a proper summation sentence can be tricky because form requires a sense of having "wrapped-up" the description, but the brevity of the description itself hardly requires a restatement of what was just said in the previous three sentences. This would result only in redundancy. But imagine if the description of the Greenbridge project simply terminated with the discussion of the roof. The reader would have been led into the cul-de-sac of detail without emerging back into consideration of the project as a whole, which should always be the logical termination point. Think of it this way: if you imagine that the project description is the jumping-off point for a discussion about it (say, at a jury or at a presentation to a client) then what do you want the next thought to be concerned with? The details of the roof assembly? Let's hope not. You want to guide the reader, jury member, or client back to a higher level of generality because you need to verify that they are on board for the overall concept of the project and the way in which it is realized. If the discussion begins with details—where the loading dock is or similarly necessary but mundane features—it is unlikely to emerge from this level and you will never know if you've succeeded at your stated goals. Thus, while the summation sentence should not be a mere restatement, it should lead the reader back out to the big issues. The Greenbridge project statement is concluded in this way:

> As the first mixed-use residential project in North Carolina to target LEED Gold, Greenbridge is poised to be a catalyst for the region and an exemplar of intelligent growth.[5]

Here, a fact concerning its being a "first" is combined with an assertion concerning its relevance for the future. Using the final sentence to place the project within a larger context is an excellent strategy. These two ideas are not merely joined, the fact of its being a "first" helps substantiate the assertion that it will become a catalyst. It's a bold assertion, but not unwarranted. No one is making such overblown claims as "This building will become a household word" or that "it shows the way of the future."

Similarly, with the description of the Wexner Center, instead of leaving the discussion at the level of skewed grids, the description guides the reader back to where the designer wants discussion to begin.

> Instead of symbolizing its function as shelter, or as a shelter for art, it acts as a symbol of art as process and idea, of the ever changing nature of art and society.[6]

What has occurred here is that the description and presentation of the project has allowed a more concrete restatement of the original premise. The project has itself acted as an argument that has made possible a further refinement of the premise. The building exemplifies a process more than it does a solution. The building itself makes this idea more plausible. This introduces the idea that if you consider the project itself as a type of argument, then the final sentence presents itself more organically to the discussion. This argument can take many forms. For the McDonough firm, the building argues for the practicality of incorporating quite substantive sustainable design features. For Eisenman, the Wexner Center argues for regarding a building, not as an end point—"A SOLUTION!"—but as a stopping point. Some buildings make arguments for a particular way of addressing street life, others for joining a crowded skyline. Some buildings argue for a certain palette of materials while others attempt to make a case that abstract theories can in fact become architecture. If you are able to ask and answer "What is YOUR building's argument?" then you will have gone a good distance toward knowing how to complete your description.

DESCRIBING YOUR WORK FOR EXTERNAL AND INTERNAL AUDIENCES

Recall from Chapter 1 that architects must write for two types of audiences—an external audience of clients, the public, contractors and the like, and an internal audience of fellow architects and others embedded in the field—and that clarity demands understanding the different presumptions of knowledge, differing standards, and divergent objectives of the two. Keeping hold of this distinction applies strongly to describing your work.

Most of the time, student design juries are composed of internal audiences; therefore, it behooves the writer to compose her descriptive text with the assumption of a reader highly knowledgeable on the subject who wants the presenter to communicate not only her decision criteria, but also her understanding of how her project fits within existing theoretical frames. What this means is that part of the description needs to include the design's provenance—how it stands in relation to important precedents. This provenance may be in relation to a theoretical context or in relation to a strand of architecture history or some combination. Peter Eisenman's description discussed earlier was clearly targeted for just this sort of audience while the description of the McDonough firm's project was more targeted to the wider public. For the external audience, provenance is usually best omitted; its more information than people can process with a limited background in the subject.

Compare the differences in descriptions of Clare Hall, referenced earlier in the chapter, between that of the architect of Clare Hall aimed at architecture's external audience and the one condensed from author Nick Ray's description aimed at those with a basic understanding of contemporary architecture history. Architect Ralph Erskine describes his "academic village" design for Clare Hall as follows:

> The buildings are grouped around two main walkways—the family walk and the dwellings, and the scholars' walk with the studies, common room and bar. Beyond these, at each

extremity of the site is a family garden and a scholars' garden. Breaking right through and across these groups is a cross-walkway . . . [allowing] a varying degree of inter-relationship between scholastic work . . . and recreation.[7]

Erskine presents a clear image of the organizational principles involved for a lay audience by using phrasal verbs such as "grouped around" and "breaking right through" and spatial prepositional phrases such as "beyond these" and "at each extremity." However, Ray targets an internal audience of connoisseurs, which expects a description originating in twentieth-century modern architecture. Ray included some spatial description, but that description serves as evidence for the ideas presented and refined at the beginning and the end of the paragraph.

Clare Hall is an example of Erskine's attempt to humanize the reductive separations of dogmatic modernism by emphasizing ideas of identity and association; qualities which such older environments as town streets and village squares possess in contrast to the aridity of many twentieth-century environments. The design displays a confidence that modern materials and inventive forms, sensitively handled, can provide as good an architecture as that of the past without resorting to stylistic imitation. Clare Hall is founded on a social model of an academic village. Two pedestrian "streets" run north-south. The eastern Scholars' Walk leads to the main social area and the dining hall. The western Family Walk is bounded by a block of flats five stories high on the north and two stories on the south. These walks are bisected by a cross walkway that connects them.[8]

The two very different descriptions do not represent right or wrong perspectives. Rather they serve different functions, each appropriate for its audience: the first passage gets right to the point of describing the underlying organizational concept while the second assumes the audience desires to understand the intellectual context out of which the design evolved (Figure 4.3).

a)

b)

FIGURE 4.3 (a) Clare Hall; and (b) Robinson College, Cambridge University, interior precincts

The design of Robinson College explores a different and, to some degree, opposing set of concerns. Here is a description for an internal audience of the design of Robinson College:

> The castle-like appearance of Robinson College results from the ongoing design exploration of the Scottish firm Gillespie, Kidd and Coia into the expressive possibilities of heavy masonry construction in a modern setting using contemporary construction technology. It exploits the thickness of masonry walls both for accommodation and for manipulation of daylight in deliberate opposition to the tendency for the exterior walls of contemporary architecture to become ever lighter and thinner. This concern for regaining a sense of solidity in expression extends to attempting to recapture a sense of collegial tradition in the building's overall organization. The college is treated as one large L-shaped building enclosing two sides of a nineteenth-century landscape. A single, portcullis-shaped entrance at the hinge-point of the L guides the visitor up, past the porter's lodge and into a linear courtyard from which all major spaces open. The plainness and severity of the courtyard contrast sharply with both the softening provided by the building's landscaped street setback as well as with the lush garden treated as a private refuge which can only be reached by moving through and across the entire building.

In this way, the architects' primary tectonic concern—overcoming the thinness of modern architecture—becomes a guiding design priority revealed to visitors and occupants alike as they approach, enter, and make use of the building. Note that while the description validates the designer's intentions, it doesn't specifically take a critical stand for or against the resulting building. Recognizing the validity of a design approach is not necessarily to endorse the results. The desired tone is one of sympathetic description—not criticism or position-taking.

Note also that the architects' specifically tectonic concern hones closely to human experience—it doesn't require extensive connoisseurship of the major themes in contemporary architecture to understand. Hence, without the sentence that refers to modern architecture's thinness, this description would be appropriate for an external audience.

COMPETITION STATEMENTS

Design statements that accompany competition entries differ from the mostly one-paragraph descriptions discussed above in that they must assume a reader with a strict agenda. The competition juror's primary expectations from the design statement are to be informed by how the project meets the competition brief and to gather a mental image—an expectation of the project's overall organization and appearance—that will inform her regard of the actual competition entry. All this must be accomplished under the severe time constraints of competition judging. Meeting the requirement of conveying a mental image is perhaps the biggest challenge for most students because, by the time they write the description after weeks of immersion in the design and preparation of the project for review, they have considerable difficulty standing back from the project, objectively evaluating the informational needs of someone completely unfamiliar with their work, and writing for that reader. All too often this results in writing that summons obvious mental images for the author but is altogether too vague for the intended reader. Consider the following composite description of a project for a family homeless shelter design competition (the sentences are numbered for ease of analysis):

> 1) There is a growing trend in homeless families. 2) Families become homeless for a variety of reasons. 3) Some suffer drug or alcohol abuse. 4) For some, it's domestic violence, while for others, economic hard times are the culprit. 5) Or it can be a combination. 6) Because of these tragedies, families may need outside help and a nurturing environment in which to rebuild. 7) That is what this shelter is designed to provide. 8) The community spaces provide social and job skills that will help overcome economic difficulties. 9) They also provide

counseling, child and health care, as all these interventions are usually needed. 10) Well-proportioned, naturally lit spaces create a soothing environment while dynamic outdoor views create excitement. 11) The dining room is the focus for the building. 12) The roof is sloped and no columns are in the space for a better scale to the room. 13) On the exterior, the building does not try to call attention to itself with jarring geometries and unusual materials, but instead seeks to fit in naturally with the surrounding neighborhood. 14) Strong brick walls symbolize security. 15) This allows the facility to bring hope for the future.

Clearly, the writer has both empathy and enthusiasm for the project, but unfortunately almost completely fails to paint even the broadest image of how the shelter is organized, what it looks like or how it is experienced. She has traded on an evocative discussion when what the reader needs is to understand the designer's logic. Heavy emphasis on the causes of family homelessness and the failure to lead into discussion of the design measures provided weaken the statement. The emphasis might have been warranted if she had connected the causes with programmatic or formal implications. A strong opening would have emphasized the architectural *response* to the program. Yes, childcare and health care spaces are provided, but *how* are they given architectural expression? Finally, there is an utter lack of development, of progression, of sentences building on one another, and of any reflective capacity on the part of the author. Let's consider the passage sentence by sentence in greater detail.

1. What the author has intimated with this awkward sentence is that within the population of homeless families, a growing trend can be discerned, when what she means to say is that the trend is actually in the growth of homeless families.

2, 3, 4, and 5. These sentences, if included at all, should be grouped into a series. Sentence 5 is not even a sentence.

6 and 7. Beginning sentence 7 with "that" is vague. Does it refer to the tragedies, the outside help, or the nurturing

environment? Clarity would be improved if these two sentences were combined so that whatever the noun "that" refers to could be the object of the sentence.

8 and 9. These two sentences merely tell the reader that the program has been provided for, but not what the architectural response to the program is.

10. One can well imagine that the author has specific places in the project in mind here, but she has failed to convey enough specificity for the reader to place these moments within an overall mental image. Furthermore, the author is in danger of creating a contradictory impression of simultaneous soothing and excitement. If both effects are operating, a sentence explaining how they can occur in concert is needed.

11. While describing an actual important space in the building is a welcome addition to the discussion, the necessary transition work has been omitted. The reader is left wondering how she suddenly showed up in the dining room.

12. Describing the details of the sloped roof and column-free interior do begin to fill in an image, but they do nothing to substantiate the claim that a better sense of scale is the result. How do these design elements do what it is claimed they do? If anything, a reader would be forgiven for thinking that the presence of columns would probably *help* establish a sense of scale residents could relate to. Again, one senses the author has a visual image in mind, only that she has not conveyed it.

13. Not only is the shift from interior to exterior appearance abrupt, but note that as the author moves to discussing the shelter's response to its immediate context, she makes the mistake of providing a negative rationale—telling us what the building *does not* do—rather than a positive one. While negative responses may in fact be strongly motivating, they only ever tell us what the author is moving away from, not what she is moving toward. Always strive to turn a negative motivator into a positive one: turn a *moving away* into a *moving toward*. Had the author written about, say, the two-story height, the brick veneer, sash windows, and cast

stone trim employed to harmonize with the surrounding buildings, a much clearer mental picture, and along with it a design rationale, would have emerged. Defining one's work in opposition to what one dislikes without an accompanying statement of what is supplied in its place only comes off sounding adolescent.

14. This is a short sentence, but with two unfortunate word choices: "strong" and "symbolize." It is a natural move to associate a sense of strength with masonry walls, which can certainly in the minds of many readers appear able to support large loads and withstand much abuse. But the fundamental fault is that the author has taken a word that should function as an adjective in this situation—"strong masonry" should refer to its superior bearing capacity over other types of wall construction—and turned it into a metaphor. What sort of strength, if not bearing capacity, does masonry symbolize? One can well imagine that what the author had in mind was a heightened sense of security that living within masonry over, say, glass, would impart to the resident, but this can only be a conjecture given what was actually written.

15. The author senses that a concluding sentence is needed, but appears so eager to wrap it up that she fails to marshal the design moves that she believes combine to substantiate the claim that hope is provided. But this sentence is not only plagued with impatience, but also vagueness. Avoid beginning a sentence with the pronoun "This" without adding a noun or series of nouns immediately following. Also vague is "hope," which is one of those words meant to elicit approval (who doesn't want more hope?) but which is also hopelessly vague in the absence of a phrase describing who is doing the hoping and what they are hoping for. Is it the resident's hope, the reader's hope, the designer's hope, or everyone's hope? Is everyone likely to share the same hope? Thus, this sentence would have to be considered vacuous as it stands. Rather than try to methodically fix this description, consider this much more organized description of the same project:

> The Homeless Assistance Center is located adjacent to and just south of the central business district. Designed specifically for the needs of homeless families, residents

would move from general assistance shelters to live here for up to eighteen months. The shelter's purpose is three fold: to provide the resources to enable parents to find regular employment, to help children return to regular schooling, and to provide a stable, safe environment necessary for families to reassemble themselves. This purpose can best be achieved when the city's institutionally provided social services are supplemented with the self-help that comes of a mutually supportive social environment amongst the shelter's residents.

The design responds to these two different sources of family renewal by providing a clear distinction between the shelter's public side and its residences. Four separate buildings—a community center and three residential buildings housing a total of 40 families—enclose and are connected by a central outdoor space. The community center's compact form allows efficient provision of services and security. It is also the shelter's "front door" which must be traversed to reach the residential units. This arrangement allows fellow residents to meet informally, securely, and in relative privacy in the cloistered outdoor spaces. Opportunities for interaction are continued inside the community center's skylit central corridor connecting its primary functions.

Though families are the fastest-growing segment of the homeless population, it remains to be seen whether shelters like this one designed specifically for families will have a large-scale impact on the problem. We have reason to hope that providing opportunities for self-help along with the expected social services will have a catalytic effect on those families that *do* enter, make use of its resources, and move back into mainstream society.

Although other formats are possible, this description illustrates that a three-part design statement is effective. First, establish the context (site, functional requirements, temporal) out of which the project arises. Second, discuss the project's premise along with some specific illustration showing how that premise is realized. Finally, conclude by reflecting on what has been learned or is likely to accrue were the project to be realized, by stating a renewed and more profound sense of the context, or by expressing a new understanding but at a higher level of abstraction. Three paragraphs will usually be needed; the second should be the longest because it does the primary work of substantiating what the design premise in the first paragraph asserts. It provides the link between the context and the implications for the reader.

This format well describes the second author's approach. The first paragraph dissects the program—it does not merely restate it. The first sentence gives a sense of the physical context while the second sentence explains the shelter's purpose. The third sentence explains the strategy behind meeting that purpose or goal—to combine social services with self-help. Paragraph two explains how the architecture reinforces this strategy. It gives a design rationale for the form and does so from the broader planning concepts employed to more specific architectural devices, such as the treatment of the central corridor. The final paragraph draws the reader back out to a more reflective attitude with a consideration of the new context that this facility will help to create. Thus, in broad strokes, we come away with a sense of the building's task as well as why the form has come to be organized in the way it has. Each sentence responds to a cue in the preceding sentence.

Perhaps just as importantly as conveying a clear sense of the project, this well-organized description gives the reader confidence in the clarity of the designer's thinking and, by association, the quality of her intelligence. Generating confidence in a client's, juror's or reviewer's mind that the design solution is both well conceived and thought through is the ultimate reward for expressing one's design ideas clearly. Never forget that the architect occupies a pivotal role in a complex and costly undertaking that requires a considerable amount of faith in the possibility of a better future. All the parties in the design and construction process are seeking in the architect someone they can be confident will see the project through to a successful realization. Your facility at writing about your own work will be one critical piece of evidence they will use to evaluate whether or not that confidence is well-placed.

exercises

Using these principles of organization, rework this building description for an external audience.

My project provides 30,000 square feet of classroom space on two floors with administration on both floors along the south façade. The building provides sustainable design features in allowing natural north-facing daylighting in all the classrooms. A large, two-story circulation spine "street" provides both the vertical and horizontal circulation as well as informal break-out space. The circulation spine breaks the building into two forms, a large classroom form on the north overlooking the recreation fields and a smaller administration block to the south facing the street. Its internal flexibility and the time-honored way it addresses the street should allow it to be a useful school building for many years to come.

Write a premise that encompasses a response to context, accounts for the functional layout, and describes all the major goals.

In the body, discuss the design measures or features that provide evidence that the design goals were in fact met. Order your sentences from most general to most specific.

Write a summation that takes the reader from the details of the design back to a reconsideration of the design within a larger context—be it the client's goals, the building's geographical location, its timeliness, a theoretical construct, or other contextual consideration.

RESEARCH REPORTS AND ANALYSES

Design is a knowledge-rich activity. So many constraints to evaluate, endless possibilities to explore! The effect can be overwhelming. Some designers react to this phenomenon of information overload by sweeping it all aside to concentrate on pure form, hoping later to be able to incorporate all the programmatic necessities without diluting their formal vision. Other designers prefer to immerse themselves in as much information as they can at the onset so as to develop an overall grasp of the space of possible design moves. Since they know that design can be as concerned with formulating interesting questions as with presenting compelling images, they do not fear too much information and aren't overly anxious to "begin designing"—that is, sketching or modeling possible forms—and instead consider their research as part of the process.

Why is research such an important part of the process? The ultimate design an architect settles on as the best solution for the occasion stands a better chance of persuading others if it appeals both to the intellect as well as to the emotions. A design which rises from a foundation of solid research acquires an authority and inspires confidence by appealing to reason whereas a design based in pure form aspires only to emotional impact. We want emotional excitement, of course, but we want to be persuaded as well.

But even more to the point, research is not a list of constraints, not just the designers' equivalent of eating your carrots, but an area that yields new considerations—in materials, in formal possibilities, in questions to ask—and ideas that the designer could not have even formulated when the design was first conceived. Research is a necessary accomplice to design. Do not hustle through it! Use it effectively to maximize its potential contribution to the design process.

OVERALL ORGANIZATION OF A REPORT

So that your design research does not devolve into a bland recitation of unrelated facts, consider the overall purpose, then organize and write to that. If you are providing research for the design team, keep in mind that most people will only consult the information produced as the need arises. They want quick access to answers to specific questions. Therefore, the report must be organized so that different people with specific questions can look for specific answers at different points in the design process. Providing interesting details that may or may not be relevant will almost certainly be wasted effort.

Even though each research section stands alone, there needs to be an overall organizational structure. A well-organized research report anticipates both the information needed and the order in which it will be accessed as the design progresses. The first order of business is to incorporate the program or brief along with an analysis. This helps set the rationale for the information to follow. If it seems logical that a designer is likely to progress from the most general to the most specific design concerns, then precedent research and site research would be the sensible opening topics. As the design gets underway, the relevant building code and disability requirements must be consulted. Once the designer has a grasp of these regulatory limitations, a logical next step is to move into considerations of massing and spatial organization. To be well integrated into a design, sustainability principles and technologies must be considered prior to making important decisions on systems. Eventually the designer is ready to move on to proposing structures, systems, exterior and interior materials. These research sections will probably be at the end.

Thus, a simple, effective organization would be:

1. Program and program analysis
2. Precedents
3. Site
4. Codes
5. Sustainability opportunities
6. Structures
7. Systems and daylighting
8. Exterior materials
9. Interior finishes

Within each section information must have a clear sense of organization as well. Your writing should be in consideration of the fact that the iterations of analysis-integration-testing that make up the design process will occur at a variety of levels of specificity. That is to say, some design ideas will be tested against constraints as broad as what is considered progressive design for the building type in the twenty-first century and others will be tested against constraints as specific as the turning radius of a wheelchair. Research should inform at both levels and everything in-between. To be useful, it must be both targeted and quickly accessible. A Google search query is quick, but targeted? It's more like an information smorgasbord; this must be avoided. In contrast to the multitude of search query hits that Google hopes will be statistically significant, the information in each section of your report must be edited and organized to anticipate specific questions the design team will ask as the design proceeds: What are the most appropriate (and "appropriate" must be defined as well) structural technologies that I should try out for the location and building type? How many exits will I need and how big must they be? What depth of overhangs and other shading devices will provide effective solar control? What floor-to-floor height is the rule of thumb for this building type? The list will go on, but the point is that research should NEVER consist of generic information, instead it should ALWAYS strive to consist of answers to specific questions. A solar chart by itself is nearly useless. A solar chart in conjunction with conclusions concerning the size of overhangs on the south façade at the project's latitude provides a real service.

Summarizing and presenting conclusions inferred from the information gathered are the researcher's major writing tasks. Write a summary for every section or subsection. Oftentimes, this is the only part that everyone can be counted on to read. The data is there to support the summary conclusions.

PROGRAM AND PROGRAM ANALYSIS

If we have a detailed program of spaces and desired functions, then what is the use of a program analysis? Why delay starting to make a building out of it? A program is an agreed-upon list of client requirements and objectives at a given point in time. Just because the list and size of spaces in a program lands on an architect's desk with an authoritative thud doesn't mean it cannot contain unrealistic expectations regarding what can be accomplished within a given space, that it doesn't overlook important spatial relationships, doesn't depart wildly from heuristic design standards, conforms to codes, or that it will not change. Therefore, before beginning the process of turning bubble diagrams into recognizable rooms with walls, a prudent designer will take the time to analyze the program and write an analysis of the results. A program analysis will highlight considerations for the project designers that may not, at first glance, be obvious. For example, though the designer will naturally attempt to accommodate every space in the program according to the space and adjacency requirements listed, what may bear emphasizing are the critical spatial relationships, the latitude in the area calculations for each space, any minimum dimensions that are likely to rule floor-to-floor heights or the ability to make planning moves.

Thus, for a hypothetical community theater, the program analysis should probably include making sure the designer understands the different work processes in the various spaces. For example, part of the program for the backstage area may call for

- Scenery production, 2000 SF
- Painting area, 200 SF (fireproofed, ventilated)

- Scenery storage, 400 SF
- Tools storage, 100 SF
- Large opening for direct transfer of scenery to stage

Research on theater design as well as such basics as *Architectural Graphic Standards* and *Time Saver Standards for Building Types* leads to the following concise analysis:

> The Scenery Production area is a full industrial workshop with its inherent workflow from delivery, to assembly, painting, placement on stage, and eventually, dismantling and storage. Workplace safety is a constant concern. Vertical "flats" are the preferred storage for lumber, backdrops, and such long materials as steel tube sections. In the painting area, a paint frame which can be raised and lowered will facilitate safety and efficiency by allowing the paint crew to avoid using ladders to reach the higher parts of the scenery. Some finished scenery will need to be stored before the stage is available for final assembly. Minimum dimensions for the doors to the stage are 16' H x 14' W. Because the production area is tall, Mezzanines over storage areas are commonly provided for offices, lockers, and further storage. Scenery production will need full communication with the front of house. Rules of thumb suggest that 400 SF of scenery storage will be inadequate and that 1000 SF is more the norm for theaters of this size.

Detailed analysis of the shop equipment, then, can be prepared in an attractive manner that combines text with graphics as in Figure 5.1.

PRECEDENTS

Because architectural design requires integration of such a variety of skills and knowledge areas, learning from precedents has traditionally been a crucial component of design education. Precedent research informs designers of the state-of-the-art as well as the classic success

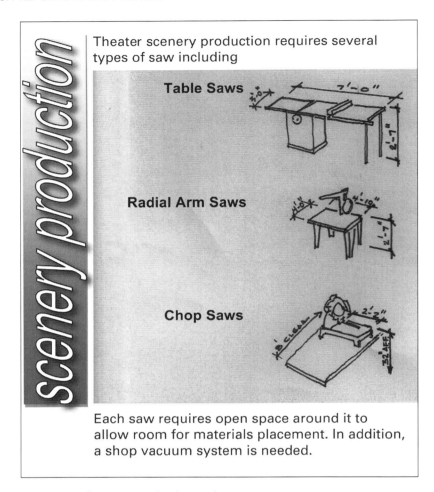

Theater scenery production requires several types of saw including

Table Saws

Radial Arm Saws

Chop Saws

Each saw requires open space around it to allow room for materials placement. In addition, a shop vacuum system is needed.

FIGURE 5.1 Scenery production tools

stories for a given building type. This knowledge will be helpful when it comes time to justify one's design approach to clients. To function most effectively, precedent research cannot be merely a mute slide show. In this respect, the products of precedent research are much like good journal entries. They combine images with statements explaining the lessons they present. The difference between precedent research and journal entries lies in the intended audience. Whereas journals are primarily for private use, precedent research always has the idea in mind that this information will be presented to others. Starting from the premise that each precedent is a response to a specific set of constraints and ideals, the written component of precedent research should explain the relevance of the precedent and the ways in which the current design task departs from it. As with the journal, notations on images are fine, but explaining the relevance and the dissimilarities requires sentences. Going beyond the private duties of the journal, however, precedent research requires not only sentences to be most useful to others, but also a summary.

For example, if we are considering using The Wyly Theatre in Dallas, Texas by OMA/Rex Architects as a precedent for a new community theater in the local community, then what needs to be shown and said about it? The unusual vertical form of the building is a direct response to the designers' intention of creating the ultimate in staging flexibility. Figures 5.2 and 5.3 illustrate.

Showing a variety of ways the theater space can be configured is a good start, but this demonstration doesn't explain *how* this flexibility was achieved, which of course is at the heart of every architect's design task. Annotated plans, sections, and diagrams will be needed to fully explain the complexity behind such an elegantly simple design goal.

Thus, in this set of images and sentences, the overall design objective, the resulting form, the means of achieving this goal, and the special requirements necessitated by the design are all explained. Both the design team and the client are efficiently guided to notice what the author considers salient. Note how much more effective the use of sentences is in this context than would be a simple note

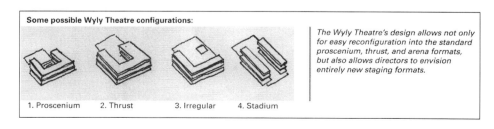

Some possible Wyly Theatre configurations:

The Wyly Theatre's design allows not only for easy reconfiguration into the standard proscenium, thrust, and arena formats, but also allows directors to envision entirely new staging formats.

1. Proscenium 2. Thrust 3. Irregular 4. Stadium

FIGURE 5.2 Wyly Theatre Configurations

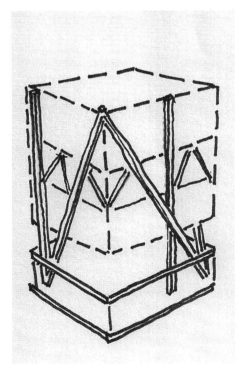

The Wyly Theatre's striking vertical form is a direct result of the design goal of providing the ultimate in staging flexibility. This is achieved by vertical stacking of functions. Note that the public entry is from underneath so as to prevent an implied stage orientation. Large diagonal braces are required to stabilize the lifting of seating sections, as well as to allow freedom at the corner

FIGURE 5.3 The Wyly Theatre, Dallas, Texas.

and arrow pointing to "diagonal braces." The note "diagonal braces" is an observation, but a sentence is a complete thought concerning the observation.

But the written component is not yet complete. Showing the precedent is only the first step of a two-stage process. The research author next needs to explain why this precedent is relevant to the task at hand, and how the current task departs from the precedent.

> No survey of contemporary theatre design would be complete without consideration of the precedent set by the Wyly. But ultimate flexibility is expensive and may not be required for our community theatre project. Our clients have asked only for a theatre design that accommodates proscenium and thrust configurations. Furthermore, our downtown site requires more attention paid to contextual responses to the immediate urban environment than was required by the culture park-like setting of the Wyly. Still, keeping in mind the unusual spatial organization of the Wyly may help us avoid making unnecessarily restrictive decisions about how a theatre must be organized.

Note that this paragraph is not intended to be architectural criticism. Again, consider the purpose, which is to address a small audience of design team members and possibly clients gathered for a specific project. Once the summary paragraph explains both the applicability and the limitations of the precedent as a model for the project at hand, its job is done.

Precedent research is not complete, however, without summarizing what is to be gleaned from the group of precedents as a whole. This is likely to include some general observations about the state-of-the-art of the building type that the precedents as a whole suggest as well as a discussion regarding the reasons behind including *these* precedents in the research report.

ANALYZING THE SITE

Site considerations merit a special analytic category as the one set of constraints that exist prior to the existence of the building as a project. Though the temptation may be to consider such site regulations as zoning and historic review requirements as of a kind with building codes (see below), they are actually conceptually and functionally different. Building code restrictions depend on building function and construction type. Zoning regulates land use; it applies whatever the building type. What do designers most need to know about the site? Primarily they will be concerned with the parameters within which they must work. Therefore, make the site research-oriented toward providing them that information.

Much of the site information architects need is best presented graphically: topography, major features, utility connections and easements, building setback requirements, traffic counts, views, sun angles, and context require little that is written, but two exceptions stand out. First, analysis of the form-giving elements of the context will highlight the important elements in the photos, drawings and diagrams (see Figure 5.4). It is one thing to have photos and drawings handy as reference, it is another to have the researcher call attention to what is *within* the photo or drawing so

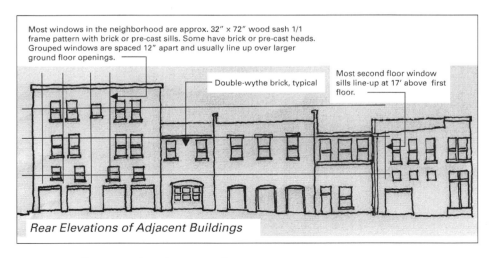

Most windows in the neighborhood are approx. 32" x 72" wood sash 1/1 frame pattern with brick or pre-cast sills. Some have brick or pre-cast heads. Grouped windows are spaced 12" apart and usually line up over larger ground floor openings.

Double-wythe brick, typical

Most second floor window sills line-up at 17' above first floor.

Rear Elevations of Adjacent Buildings

FIGURE 5.4 Documenting site research

the reader can reflect on it. For example, in the theater project mentioned above, researchers thought it important to call designers' attention to the patterns of window placement in adjacent buildings. What was produced bears much in common with a journal entry.

The second exception is that a conclusion should be reached regarding the site features most likely to influence design decisions. There is no point to writing an abbreviated discussion of everything in the site analysis. The following paragraph contains an effective conclusion:

> In conclusion, two major site concerns emerge. Almost all the patrons will arrive to the site from the parking areas to the southeast yet a strong southeastern orientation to the building will cause it to turn its back on the main part of the downtown area to the west. Therefore, the building orientation must address both directions. The second major consideration derives from the zoning height restriction. Fitting the building within the 30′ height limit will be difficult, especially since the high water table means that a full basement is impractically expensive.

Within a few sentences, attention is called to the site constraints that will do the most to limit the space of possible design moves. By omission, it is telling the reader that accommodating historic review, utilities, and the rest will be a straightforward process.

ANALYZING CODES AND STANDARDS

Code research not only identifies the sections applicable to the project, but it goes further and actually makes at least a first run at performing the calculations that determine allowable height and areas, number of exits, corridor width, and provision of toilet facilities. Since these conclusions will almost assuredly be recalculated as the design progresses, part of the findings should include procedures for performing calculations (calculating egress width, for example) along with an example of actually performing the calculation. Do not be satisfied with merely providing a reference to a code section. At minimum, the researcher should include the occupancy types from Chapter 3 of the *International Building Code*, construction types from Chapter 6 (Table 601 is especially important), height and area restrictions drawn from Chapter 5 (especially the crucial Table 503), egress requirements specific to the project from Chapter 10 (Table 1004: floor area allowances per occupancy type is especially important), required toilet facilities drawn from Table 2902 of the IBC Plumbing Code, and accessibility requirements drawn from Title III of the *Americans With Disabilities Act* in the United States and the *Americans with Disabilities Act and Architectural Barriers Act Accessibility Guidelines*, United States Access Board.

For example, for the theater project, the code summary was as in Figure 5.5.

Making the code summary into a spreadsheet will aid in automatically recalculating totals as the design evolves—as functional elements are added or deleted, the programmed sizes of various spaces are found to be lacking or too generous—and as early assumptions are discarded.

A paragraph of conclusions is in order in the presentation of codes and standards as well. As with the site research, the designers need to know, most of all, what the major limitations on their design options will be.

> Fire protection in the flyloft above the stage is always a crucial design determinant. Scenery production is considered medium-hazard factory work which will need to be kept within its own fire-rated walls so as not to require expensive separations within the lower hazard business areas. Egress from the seating area will be closely checked and only half of it can exit through the lobby.

This should be sufficient to call designers' attention to what the researcher anticipates will be the thorniest code issues.

Programmed Space	Occu- pancy Category	Code Section	Area	Occupants Per S. F. (table 1004)	Number of occupants
Theater seating	A-1	303	8000	8 SF/person Fixed seating	1000
Stage	A-1	303	2400	15	160
Lobby/ Gallery	A-3	303	5000	5	1000
Green Room	A	303	180	15	12
Rehearsal Room	A	303	2400	15	160
Dressing Rooms	B	304	1000	50	20
Costume Production	B	304	800	200	4
Offices	B	304	500	100	5
Kitchen	B	304	300	100	3
Scenery Production	F	306	2000	200	10
Technical Storage	S-1	311	1500	300	5
Back of Stage	S-1	311	1000	300	4
Coat Check	S-2	311	60	300	1
Mechanical		311	2100	300	7
Totals			**27,240**		**2391**

FIGURE 5.5 Code summary chart

SUSTAINABILITY

For the greatest effectiveness, sustainability objectives should be incorporated into the research as part of the overall design strategy and not as mitigating techniques applied after the design is largely complete. If the client is interested in the project's achieving some sort of sustainability certificate (such as LEED in the United States or BREEAM in the U.K.), then it would make sense to organize the information along the section designations of one of those standards. In the case of LEED, that would mean the following organization:

Pervious paving

Pervious concrete paving is a promising sustainability technique for this site which can address LEED sections 6.1 and 6.2 "Stormwater Design—Quantity and Quality Control" by reducing stormwater runoff and by reducing the solids that do runoff the site. The concept of pervious concrete is to deliberately create pavement with sufficient voids to allow 3–8 gallons of stormwater per square foot per minute to percolate through and down to the ground rather than travel across the surface to the stormwater piping system. Installing pervious concrete requires trained and certified installers who understand the technology. First of all, the site must be made fairly level to discourage water from running across the site before seeping through. Flattening the parking lot to discourage runoff is counter to conventional design and will require some education for the civil engineer. Once the site is leveled, a 6" layer of gravel is spread and then the pervious concrete is poured in sections 5–6" thick. The concrete can be tinted if desired, but to create the voids, the mix is very dry with little sand resulting in an overall consistency that looks more like rice crispy treats than it will a hard smooth surface. Though the roughness of the surface may be considered an aesthetic limitation, it can be a good thing for natural slip-resistance. Because the site is flattened to encourage absorption and because the concrete and gravel contain significant voids, pervious pavement actually decreases runoff when compared to grass and other ground cover. Not only does the paving reduce runoff rates, but because of the voids constitute between 15–20% of the volume of both the concrete and the graded gravel aggregate it can actually be calculated as part of the stormwater detention generated by the impervious elements on the site—thus reducing the size of any detention ponds. Due to the special nature of the concrete mix and the resultant care required for installation, pervious concrete is roughly double that of conventional concrete paving.

Above: Pervious concrete sections in this parking lot help control runoff.
Right: Pervious concrete absorbing poured water.

FIGURE 5.6 Report on Sustainability Strategies

1. Sustainable Sites
2. Water Efficiency
3. Energy and Atmosphere
4. Materials and Resources
5. Indoor Environmental Quality
6. Innovation in Design
7. Regional Priority

Note the sample sustainability section on pervious paving in Figure 5.6. The first task it addresses is purpose. It establishes the sustainability objectives that using this type of paving would help meet. Virtually all the questions a designer would need to answer to choose this technology (special design considerations that depart from ordinary concrete paving, aesthetic considerations, and benefits vs. costs) are covered. It discusses the potential benefits for stormwater management that the technology provides, but foregoes providing the actual methodology for calculation because those calculations are made by consulting engineers and not architects. It does, however, provide the rationale for discussing those calculations with consultants. Neither does the discussion waste the designer's attention with information that every designer should already know or is too technical for the design phase. For example, it does discuss that the concrete mix is drier and contains less sand than conventional concrete. However, it doesn't overwhelm with such details as the slump test either, which will eventually become important in writing the specifications, but at this juncture would simply hinder digesting the design considerations.

STRUCTURES

The structures research in school will be broader and more generic than in practice because, in practice, the recommendations of the structural engineering consultant will be incorporated early in the design process whereas in studio it is reasonable to assume that students will be experimenting with a wide variety of approaches. Along with 1) providing diagrams and illustrations, the structures research should 2) discuss the design live and dead loads, 3) give the rules of thumb for span-to-depth ratio of different systems, and 4) make recommendations for the most plausible structural systems for the construction type (I–V) required to meet code. Making sure that the structures research satisfies these four requirements should make it useful but not exhaustive. Figure 5.7 illustrates a page out of a simple structures report.

SYSTEMS AND DAYLIGHTING

Under the "systems" heading is the appropriate place for research on mechanical, electrical, lighting, and plumbing systems (customarily the eventual province of the mechanical engineering consultant), as well as any other unusual systems that need to be given design consideration. For example, daylighting, security, and noise reduction systems might fit into this category. Most of the information will be graphic and diagrammatic, but descriptions of different systems and conclusions will be written. As always, drawing and reporting conclusions in a straightforward manner should be the ultimate goal, as in the following example.

> Mechanical System Conclusions: The theater building will require two entirely different mechanical systems, a low-velocity constant air volume (CAV) system for the performance space primarily to maximize sound control, and a variable air volume (VAV) system for the remainder of the building. Large exhaust systems must be accommodated in the shop areas. Fan rooms must be located at least 100' from the performance spaces and diffusers chosen for their noise reduction coefficients (NRC) in the performance space.

Sometimes the purpose of research isn't so much to help make initial decisions, as with the mechanical systems, as it is to help expand designers' thinking of the possibilities, as in Figure 5.8. Daylighting strategies are particularly amenable to this approach because they can so significantly impact a building's aesthetic

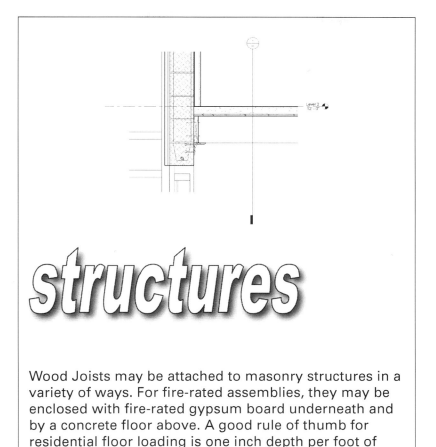

Wood Joists may be attached to masonry structures in a variety of ways. For fire-rated assemblies, they may be enclosed with fire-rated gypsum board underneath and by a concrete floor above. A good rule of thumb for residential floor loading is one inch depth per foot of span. Commercial loadings will require more depth. Wood joists may be used for Type III or Type V construction, both protected and unprotected.

FIGURE 5.7 Report on Structures Research

SHADING STRATEGIES

These three images each display different approaches to sunlight control. On the left a sleek appearance is preserved with internal blinds giving individual users maximum control over the amount of sunlight they wish to allow in. This system has the disadvantage of being thermally inefficient since solar heat gain entering the building must still be overcome by the mechanical system. In the second image, a western exposure is countered with vertically aligned exterior metal "blinds." The southwest angle and the staggered placement of these shading devices will intercept much of the undesirable western sun. A highly expressive appearance is achieved on the south façade of the third building with exterior metal shades juxtaposed at a variety of angles and densities but which achieve, overall, a high shading coefficient.

FIGURE 5.8 Report on Shading Strategies

appearance. Thus, for example, three different daylight control strategies are shown in Figure 5.8. This could serve as the starting point for discussing the relative advantages and disadvantages of each strategy.

MATERIALS

The possibilities for interior and exterior materials are so many and various that it would be pointless to engage in much research until after the schematic design phase. Only after the schematic design phase is the character of the building sufficiently understood that a materials palette to support the overall concept can be fruitfully narrowed into first and alternate choices. Thus, the materials research is usually engaged subsequent to the rest.

Eventually, however, a materials list approaching the status of a report in its own right should be developed and organized according to the fourteen-part Construction Specifications Institute divisions. A material is usefully considered as just another technology, and so the materials reports should answer the same basic questions as the others: What is the idea behind using this product? How is it assembled? What are its benefits, limitations, and unit cost? Accompanying this information with an image and an assembly diagram will generally complete a section of materials research.

It should be clear from the examples in this chapter that research and analysis requires considerably more than the accumulation and organization of data: these tasks continually exercise the writer's judgment to sift through the alternatives and make recommendations. Research and analysis incorporates a recognizable process that generally begins with targeted data gathering. Recommendations emerging from this data will be used to help form evolving design goals to keep the project within the realm of the possible. When done poorly, it will seem like busy work. When executed succinctly—with the design tasks ahead uppermost in mind—it will not only expedite the design process but also provide it with a solid empirical footing.

exercises

1. Choose a material or technology you want to learn more about. Photograph it and describe its advantages and drawbacks.

2. Go to the sections of the International Building Code referred to earlier in the chapter to complete this table for a restaurant project, and then write a one-paragraph narrative discussing the most important code considerations.

Programmed Space	Occu-pancy Category	Code Section	Area	Occupants Per S. F. (table 1004)	Number of occupants
Waiting			150		
Dining room seating			3000		
Bar			600		
Restrooms			200		
Private dining room			500		
Kitchen			2000		
Receiving			200		
Loading dock			200		
Dry goods storage			200		
Cold storage			150		
Totals			7200		

BUSINESS DOCUMENTS

Marketing brochures, proposals, business plans and the like share similarities with technical writing—they both seek objectivity and clarity—but they incorporate two important differences. First and foremost, business writing is aimed at an external audience of potential clients, lenders, and members of the public who will be affected by the architect's actions. Unlike engineers, code officials and contractors, this audience is likely to be unfamiliar with much of the technical jargon of the industry and therefore will be alienated by use of extremely discipline-specific words. Achieving a confident, yet friendly, tone should be the goal. A balance must be sought: overconfidence may be perceived as boastful, authoritarian or self-absorbed while an overly friendly tone risks being perceived as ingratiating or too folksy to be taken seriously. Emanating from this recognition of the difference in the intended audience is the second important difference: understanding that in this context you are writing for people who have the power to enable or hinder your actions. Therefore, you are frankly seeking to convince them of something, perhaps that your business model is sound and therefore you deserve a loan, or that the building you propose will benefit the community and therefore the planning board should approve it, or that you have the necessary experience and are the best person for the job. In this context of persuasive writing, expressing one's idealism is allowed but it should always be illustrated with tangible examples. Business writing succeeds best when the reader comes away not only well informed about the author's intentions, but also with a comforting sense of the author herself. Those in the position of granting a loan, approving a project, or hiring a firm will be reassured in their favorable decision if, along with approval of the plan, they also gain trust in the person putting it forward. Your business writing will often be the first opportunity a client, a loan committee, or a planning board has to evaluate the person doing the writing.

MARKETING

For obvious reasons, your marketing often precedes all other forms of contact. Joe M. Powell's book *The New Competitiveness in Design and Construction: 12 Strategies That Will Drive the 21st-century's Most Successful Firms* provides a good overview of the marketing process for architects and others concerned with the provisioning of building.[1] Architects should resist the notion that marketing is a matter of selling people something they don't need. A more useful attitude is that marketing is a process beginning with self-identification that leads to matching up what you can provide with those who might benefit from knowing about you. At its best, marketing is a meeting of equals. At its worst, it is a supplicant attempting to secure favor from his superiors. All successful marketing is based on innovative research. Out of this research will emerge a guiding concept—a design—for a firm's marketing. While the marketing plan may well be strictly internal to the organization and therefore under its control, the eventual marketing materials employed to spread the word about yourself will radiate in ways that cannot be fully anticipated.

The Mission Statement

The first part of a marketing effort should be a mission statement. (Call it what you will: "Statement of Purpose," "About Us," "Our Philosophy.") The mission statement has something of a dubious reputation because there are so many inept ones that either fail to capture the true spirit of the organization they seek to represent, or else capture all-too-well the confused or bland self-image of the firm. As a first step in self-definition, as well as in ultimately inspiring confidence from outsiders, a good mission statement is highly useful.

Here's a portion of what the New York firm Pei Cobb Freed Partners (Figure 6.1) has to say about itself:

> Although the firm's practice over the past five decades has been exceptionally diverse in terms of building type and setting, a central theme consistently evident in its built works is the conception of architecture as an art of place making—an art embodying above all else a concern for the quality of public space and public life.[2]

Note that the firm chooses one theme—the art of place making—to explain its fundamental orientation. Clearly, this might scare off some potential clients who aren't interested in building something that, in addition to solving functional needs, also responds and contributes to a sense of place, and this is alright with

FIGURE 6.1 A project designed by Pei Cobb Freed Partners, The San Francisco Public Library

the firm; it is not interested in attracting mercenary projects so it might as well dispense at the outset with clients with which it is a poor fit.

This statement from BNIM Architects of Kansas City accomplishes an even more concise job of self-definition:

> With the support of our visionary clients, BNIM is working to redefine the realm of green planning and design.[3]

In just one sentence the firm conveys how it seeks to differentiate itself from the pack and it does so in accessible language. Now, a potential client may not especially want green design and may well be intimidated by the thought of becoming visionary, but nothing in the way the statement itself is assembled is alienating. Its straightforwardness, which extends to its expression in the first person possessive "our" rather than the third person, may, in fact, be intriguing to some potential clients.

Vague or bland statements of purpose are counterproductive to one's marketing goals. When Firm A's lead is on the order of "We are dedicated to client service" or Firm B's lead is a series of feel-good words "Excellence. Trust. Service," then the potential client has been given extra work to do to decode such messages. *Is* Firm A really going to slavishly work to satisfy the client's needs and nothing else or is it just deliberately saying something ingratiating about itself so as not to alienate anyone? *Do* Firm B's words mean anything at all or are they merely meant to elicit an approving attitude from all comers? This is the problem with statements that traffic in generic or vague messages about themselves: they oblige interested potential clients to take the extra step of figuring out what they REALLY mean. Being forced to decode a firm's marketing message introduces a layer of suspicion. Why not simply say what you are about at the outset unless you are afraid of being direct? Marketing's process of self-definition and positioning entails the recognition that one can never be all things to all people.

Initially, and understandably, firms or interns seeking work may resist boiling-down what they stand for into a sentence or two. "I'm much more multi-dimensional than that!" they will be tempted to think. This is undoubtedly true, and your mother will agree, but such an attitude doesn't solve the essential problem that you are trying to help strangers quickly grasp what differentiates you from the architect down the block or at the next table. (Actually, your mom could probably very quickly point out one or two things that make you unique.) Consider your mission statement a design problem, which, like all design problems, must have a fundamental generating idea to guide all subsequent statements. Even a bull-riding, tuba-playing attorney and father of seven will have *something* that connects all these apparently unrelated pieces of his life. Perhaps, as a student or intern, your truth is that you are very much a work in the process of becoming and you are simply unable to say what it is that makes you unique. At least *that* is a solid observation around which you can then explain what you have done and are doing to figure out what you stand for. If all you can say about yourself is that you are just muddling through, then hopefully you have family connections.

A well-chosen mission statement will help guide all further marketing materials toward creating a consistent statement about the firm. A firm cannot emphasize its "commitment to design excellence" in its mission and then show a series of bland projects without inducing a cognitive break in the reader. It cannot tell of its "dedication to the building user" and only show photos of uninhabited buildings without risking the same. The truth is that it's a rare project indeed that only one firm is supremely qualified to handle. Therefore, when interviewing and ranking firms for projects, clients are, of necessity, looking for reasons to eliminate some. Inconsistencies in one's presentation are easy to catch, quickly lead to doubts and uncertainties in the mind of the reader, which become reasons in themselves for disqualification.

Project Descriptions

No convincing marketing effort can go without showing evidence of prior work, and no showing of prior work should be presented without a paragraph discussing it. It is simply not plausible that you would have spent months or years on a project yet have nothing interesting to say about it. The same principles should apply here as they do to the mission statement. An authoritative yet friendly tone combined with enthusiasm for one's work, clarity of description, and a sense of the persons behind the project are the elements of a successful discussion. An anecdote or a personal moment always makes for a good introduction to a project—but beware that the discussion does not become all anecdote lest it succumb to "cute." There should always be something about each project that jumps out: "The Landmark office building went from design to construction completion in just 12 months." Or "The Northwest Fire House ultimately won the Fire Station of the Year Award." Or "This project led to our client's selecting us for her next two projects." Or "Suburban office buildings like the Landmark Building are central to our practice." Or "In this project we developed further our fascination with using off-the-shelf building components in innovative ways." If you are showing it as part of your marketing, then there has to be some reason for doing so. State it. If you can think of no ways to differentiate yourself in a market economy, then that only leaves competition by price.

Project descriptions on architects' websites and in their other marketing materials are oftentimes unfortunately analytic: "The Norfolk Tower is a 120,000 Square Foot Office building in suburban Atlanta built in 2005," or even reduced to a set of bullet points:

- Project: Norfolk Tower
- Size: 120,000 SF
- Location: Suburban Atlanta
- Year built: 2005

Both strategies are at odds with the essential purpose of marketing: to be persuasive. The basic problem is that this approach introduces a discordant analytic dryness in a writing opportunity to convey an emotionally informed message. At such junctions, the reader is left unsure whether the firm is so self-unaware that it doesn't know what to say about its own work, or else is guided by fear of alienating a potential client by saying the wrong thing. Neither perception is desirable to instill in a reader. At best, such documentation strategies tell of the firm's competence to design something similar. Rather than allow the reader to arrive, unguided, at her own conclusions, seek to call her attention to something about the building worth noticing.

For example, the Seattle firm Callison says just enough about its FlatIron Crossing retail project in Bloomfield, Colorado to communicate its justifiable pride in the project's commercial success, but without making empty boasts:

> Callison's innovative plan for FlatIron Crossing launched a new retail destination model, combining a two-level enclosed mall and an open-air town center. With an identity, design and amenities that respond to the community's outdoor lifestyle, cultural aspirations and sensitivity to the environment, FlatIron Crossing emanates a sense of place that is a true community asset.[4]

Note that the first sentence of the description makes the assertion that the design is "innovative" and then quickly, within the same sentence, supports that assertion by stating how that innovation is achieved. This makes the assertion of "innovation" meaningful. The second sentence also contains an assertion—that the project has become a community asset—but in this case the assertion comes as the result of the description preceding. Both strategies for backing-up one's assertions are legitimate; only be sure that you do, indeed, back them up.

Clearly the firm in this case is placing the most emphasis on its ability to facilitate market success, but project descriptions need not be so business-oriented even if the client is a business. For example, Omaha's Randy Brown Architects begins discussion of an advertising agency project with a generalized observation:

> A familiar object seen in an unfamiliar context can become perceptually new as well as old.[5]

FIGURE 6.2 Borrowing from the rural environment

After making this observation, the project statement avoids becoming an empty generalization by explaining how this idea was given architectural form (Figure 6.2):

> The design borrows materials from the rural environment, using corrugated metal, galvanized buckets, bluestem grasses and plumbing pipe in new and unexpected ways.[6]

This change in emphasis reflects not only the differences between the projects but, more significantly, also the cultural differences between the two firms.

Descriptions of projects can be as diverse as the projects themselves, except that erring on the side of brevity is always more desirable than long-windedness. In any case, the description should answer the question: Why show this project? The individual project description should, then, lead back into the discussion of the firm's overall design approach. This overall project statement should explain how each project differs (other than in size and location) from the other projects shown and how continuity is achieved. Both continuity and uniqueness can be desirable qualities in a firm, yet whichever one is emphasized, potential clients will want to know how the other is addressed. Too much individuality between projects without some explanation for the underlying similarities—the firm's approach, perhaps—will run the risk of making the firm appear rudderless. Too much continuity leads to fears of staleness, cookie-cutter design, and lack of artistry. If continuity is emphasized, the firm will need to explain the important differences between projects as well. This work is all part of the ongoing self-definition process of marketing.

The Proposal

Significant parts of both proposals and business plans often require little to no composing. They consist of filling out forms, such as the General Services Administration Form *SF330 Architect-Engineer Qualifications*, or a lender's financial statement, so that the agency can objectively compare qualifications or so that the lender can compute credit-worthiness according to its benchmarks. But less bureaucratic clients will want to see at least a cover letter composed and tailored to its specific project. The cover letter should generally include a statement about the firm: its design philosophy, its experience, and its ability to take on the project under consideration. Virtually every firm making its sales pitch will discuss its devotion to client service, its track record for delivering projects on time and on budget, its wonderful and experienced people, and its belief in the value of good design. These topics have become so commonplace that it is no longer possible to rephrase them to distinguish your firm's proposal from any other.

At this point a decision is required. The firm may elect to take a passive approach, minimize its investment in the proposal, and hope to win its statistical share against other similarly qualified firms. If this is the chosen course of action, then the cover letter is a formality that establishes who at the firm has taken responsibility for project procurement. Alternatively, the firm can invest some extra time in research with the idea in mind that such research will help generate one or two fresh—and project-specific—discussion topics that it can incorporate into its statement to both demonstrate its enthusiasm as well as begin to engage the client in its thought process. For example, in its cover letter for a university classroom building project, a firm explained how in a similar building it worked early on with the mechanical engineer to maximize natural ventilation techniques resulting in lower utility bills, smaller ductwork, and a reduced mechanical room. Based on its analysis of the program, the firm believed that similar economies could be had for the proposed building. No organization is going to reject out-of-hand the prospect of lower construction and operating costs, especially not from a firm that meets the basic requirements in all other respects. In this case, the cover letter becomes much more than a formality. It takes advantage of the one occasion the firm can be *sure* its marketing message will actually be read by a potential client to begin to engage it in the design process.

If the firm has already prepared its marketing materials, then completing the qualifications statement within the overall proposal should come naturally as a direct outgrowth of its marketing.

TECHNICAL WRITING: SPECIFICATIONS AND FIELD REPORTS

The Specifications

The typical contract for construction includes the contract agreement itself and the General Conditions of the Contract, which spell out in great detail the expected roles of all the parties; the construction drawings; and the specifications. Drawings and specifications complement each other. While drawings are the preferred mode for indicating the location and quantity of the work, text-based specifications are the first line of defense for insuring the desired quality. Nowhere else but in the specifications can the required construction tolerances, the product names and numbers, the conditions under which products may be safely applied, the work that must be coordinated with the product, the required warranties, and the relevant testing standards be elaborated. Specifications are not requests; they are sets of instructions concerning materials and installation techniques. As such, they must be written in precise and unambiguous language. While in other contexts contractors may bristle at being told explicitly what to do and how to do it, when it comes to the specifications they will appreciate precision and directness.

To specify every product and material within a building is a substantial undertaking easily resulting in a document the size of a metropolitan phone book. To ease the task of writing such a document from scratch, there are four alternatives. The firm may

- Hire specification writers for a fee.
- Edit and update an existing spec instead of writing a completely new specification for each project.
- Use automated specification-writing software now available as an add-on to Building Information Modeling programs such as Revit.
- Use manufacturer-formatted specifications in electronic format to make it more convenient for architects to specify their products.

Hiring a qualified specification writer is almost certainly the safest alternative, but also the most expensive. Updating an existing specification is a common practice, but is susceptible to specifying out-of-date or no longer available products or worse—products which aren't in the building at all—leaving the contractor scratching his head and possibly including a cost line for a product that isn't even intended. Automated specifications, unless every piece of the building is modeled, may leave things out. They too must be carefully edited by someone intimately familiar with the project. The pre-formatted manufacturers' specifications merit special scrutiny as they will likely be written to exclude the possibility of using competitors' products, often for no good reason. Since every shortcut has its liabilities, there is really no easy way out; one may as well do the best job possible. A specification can be either proprietary, descriptive, performance-based, or some combination of the three. Proprietary specifications, also called prescriptive specifications, indicate specific products, vendors, and even, possibly, installers that are acceptable. A "closed" proprietary specification allows only one product by one manufacturer to be acceptable. An "open" proprietary specification will list more than one acceptable product, or at the least leave the door open for consideration of alternatives if proposed by the contractor. The obvious reason to prefer an open to a closed specification is cost competition amongst manufacturers. Governmental entities will usually not allow closed specifications.

Two competing ways of formatting specifications exist, and they each have their uses. The CSI/Masterspec format organizes divisions in order of material. Thus concrete products are division 3, masonry, division 4, metals are in division 5, wood and plastics belong to division 6, and so on. The Uniformat system (also developed by CSI) recognizes that architectural elements are rarely conceived solely by individual material. Instead, they are conceived of and installed as assemblies, systems, or layers of different materials all acting together to produce a desired outcome. This is a much more logical way for architects to group the products that need to work in concert in an exterior wall, for example. Furthermore, *Means Cost Guides* lists linear or area costs of various assemblies, thus making it much simpler to develop good cost estimates and to consider the costs of alternates. The computer modeler Revit also references assemblies in their Uniformat number to enable dynamic cost estimating of various building components with the help of *Means*. In the Uniformat system, Division A is substructure, Division B shell, Division C Interiors, Division D services, Division E equipment and furnishings. After each letter prefix, a long number follows to isolate the particular assembly. This assembly number can be tied to pricing information, as well as specification information. The Uniformat system is conceived primarily for developing preliminary data and cost, while the more extensive CSI Masterspec is conceived of as providing a more complete and exhaustive specification. (For more information on formatting specifications refer to www.csinet.org.)

Regardless of overall format, standard organization of the information within a particular specification calls for dividing it into three parts to ease information retrieval by contractors and subcontractors: Part 1 is general information pertaining to the product (if samples are required, warranties and the like). In Part 2 the product and acceptable alternates are described in detail. Part 3 discusses the necessary installation procedures.

Not all lines in a specification require sentences. But where sentences calling for action by the contractor are used, they should be written in the imperative mood. The easiest way to think in the imperative mood is to start each sentence with a verb. For example:

- "Install at no less than 50 degrees Farenheit."
- "Provide manufacturer's 20-year warranty."
- "Overlap splice joints a minimum of 6 inches."

Note: There is no need to start sentences with "The Contractor. . ." as it is assumed that the contractor is the intended reader.

The imperative mood keeps the writing direct and economical. Placing the required action at the front of each sentence benefits the contractor seeking clarity, but it also disciplines the architect to think at each turn "What exactly do I want to say here?"

The following common words or phrases that can cause confusion in specifications if not used properly:

- Shall vs. Will: "Shall" designates a command where "Will" implies a choice. Most likely "Shall" is the proper word choice for a specification.
- Either: The word "Either" implies that there is a choice between either one or the other. The word "Both" may be a more descriptive word choice.
- Amount: "Amount" is a term that should be used to refer to money. "Quantity" is the appropriate word to use for construction materials.
- Any vs. All: "Any" implies a choice. "All" is a more prescriptive and exact choice of words.

DIVISION 9 – FINISHES
SECTION 09250 GYPSUM BOARD ASSEMBLIES
PART 1 GENERAL

1.01 SUMMARY

A. Provide gypsum board assemblies:
1. Interior walls, partitions, and ceilings.
2. Steel framing systems to receive gypsum board.
3. Vapor barrier systems in gypsum board assemblies.

B. Gypsum Board Attachment:
1. Screw attached to steel framing and furring.

1.02 SUBMITTALS

A. Submit for approval product data and mock up of typical partition for approval of materials and finish, 8 feet high by 8 feet long.

1.03 QUALITY ASSURANCE

A. Comply with governing codes and regulations.
Provide products of acceptable manufacturers which have been in satisfactory use in similar service for three years. Use experienced installers. Deliver, handle, and store materials in accordance with manufacturer's instructions.

B. Tolerances: Not more than 1/16 inch difference in true plane at joints between adjacent boards before finishing. After finishing, joints shall be not be visible. Not more than 1/8 inch in 10 feet deviation from true plane, plumb, level and proper relation to adjacent surfaces in finished work.

C. Fire Resistance for Fire Rated Assemblies: ASTM E 119.

D. Performance: Fire performance meeting requirements of building code and local authorities.

PART 2 PRODUCTS

2.01 MATERIALS

A. Acceptable Manufacturers of Gypsum Board: Georgia Pacific Corp., National Gypsum Co., United States Gypsum Co. or approved equal.

B. Acceptable Manufacturers of Steel Framing and Furring: Dietrich Industries, National Gypsum Co., or approved equal.

C. Gypsum Board:
1. Gypsum Wallboard: ASTM C 36, fire rated type, 5/8 inch typical thickness.
2. Water Resistant Gypsum Backing Board: ASTM C 630, regular type, 5/8 inch typical thickness.

FIGURE 6.3 A typical three-part specification section

3. Joint Treatment: ASTM C 475 and ASTM C 840, 3 coat system, paper or fiberglass tape.
D. Trim Accessories:
1. Material: Metal or plastic trim.
2. Types: Corner bead, edge trim, and control joints.
E. Steel Framing for Walls and Partitions:
1. Steel Studs and Runners: ASTM C 645, 25 gauge (.0179 inch) steel studs, 3⅝ inch typical depth with manufacturer's standard corrosion resistant coating.
2. Furring Channels: ASTM C 645, 25 gauge (.0179 inch) with manufacturer's standard corrosion resistant coating.
3. Auxiliary Framing Components: Furring brackets, resilient furring channels, and non corrosive fasteners.
F. Auxiliary Materials:
1. Gypsum board screws, ASTM C 1002.
2. Adhesive.
3. Polyethylene vapor retarder, 6 mils. thickness.

PART 3 EXECUTION

3.01 INSTALLATION

A. Install steel framing in compliance with ASTM C 754. Install with tolerances necessary to produce substrate for gypsum board assemblies with tolerances specified. Include blocking for items such as railings, grab bars, casework, toilet accessories and similar items.
B. Install gypsum board assemblies in compliance with ASTM C 840 and GA 216, Recommended Specifications for the Application and Finishing of Gypsum Board. Install gypsum board assemblies true, plumb, level and in proper relation to adjacent surfaces.
C. Provide fire rated systems where indicated and where required by authorities having jurisdiction.
D. Install boards horizontally. All joints must occur at framing members.
E. Install trim and 3 coat joint treatment in compliance with manufacturer's instructions. Install joint treatment at all fasteners and edges. Fill all surface defects. Sand after each joint treatment coating and leave ready for finish painting or wall treatment.

****** END OF SECTION 9250 – GYPSUM BOARD ASSEMBLIES *****

- Etc.: This is ambiguous by nature and should not be used in specification writing.

Figure 6.3 shows an example of a proprietary specification for a gypsum board specification in a hypothetical building if the specification is organized, as many are, according to the Construction Specifications Institute division format.

Note that the end of each section and each division is deliberately labeled. This is done as part of the larger strategy to avoid vagueness or ambiguity.

Descriptive specs attempt to determine the desired characteristics of the product or assembly and then let anyone who can meet those requirements submit a product for consideration.

A descriptive specification for carpeting, for example, would include:

- Construction type (tufted, woven, etc.)
- Pile yarn (olefin, nylon, wool, etc.)
- Gauge or pitch (thickness of the yarn)
- Stitches per inch
- Pile height
- Colorization method (solution dyed, silkscreen, etc.)
- Number of plies
- Yarn weight
- Backing material
- And possibly a reference standard such as ASTM, UL, ASHRAE

This is obviously a lot to know about a piece of carpet and can take quite a bit of research to adequately describe.

Performance specs are similar to descriptive specs in that they do not list products by name, but instead of trying to fully describe a product's physical characteristics, they seek to encapsulate the performance that the designer is seeking from the product. For example, a layer of sound-reduction material between apartment units might be specified as "Meets sound attenuation reduction of 25 db and provides a minimum R-value of 13."

Meeting Notes

During the course of a project, the demand on the architect's ability to communicate rarely ends with the drawings and specifications. Such tasks as summarizing construction meetings, evaluating contractors' pay requests, generating approval of changes during construction, and verifying construction progress for lenders will all require concise written documentation. For most of these tasks, the demand is primarily on the architect's powers of organization and not on her ability to construct a written narrative (Figure 6.4).

FIGURE 6.4 Construction necessitates meeting notes

The purpose of meeting notes is to establish common agreement on the project's progress toward completion and to identify potential trouble spots that could hinder this progress. They are distributed to all involved parties; therefore, they demonstrate the architect's skill at clearly organizing observations and summarizing discussions. The typical format documents the attendees, the progress since the last meeting, anticipation of major work before the next meeting, the topics discussed, the decisions made, and the delegation of new responsibilities. The description of the progress of construction might be organized as a paragraph, but it can often be as easily and as well organized as a list.

For example, as a narrative

The architect, project manager, mechanical engineer, and client met on Tuesday, March 4 at the contractor's job trailer. At this point in time, the structural frame is 100% complete, the roofing is complete, exterior walls are nearing completion with 2/3 of the doors and windows installed, the mechanical system is roughed-in, metal stud walls are mostly installed, the electrical wiring has begun, and the sanitary plumbing rough-in is complete. The Contractor showed the work progress against the Critical Path chart was on time. Drywall installation is set to begin on March 11 and last for three weeks. The client expressed concern that the size of the ductwork in Classroom A and in Offices 10, 11, and 12 has lowered the ceilings beyond what was called for in the plans. Various alternatives were discussed. The mechanical engineer will review his calculations, discuss the matter with the mechanical contractor and see if a recommendation can be made to revise the duct profile. This concluded the meeting.

Or as a list as shown in Figure 6.5.

As desirable as the ability to craft well-constructed paragraphs is in other contexts, in this context the list format is clearly preferable. Why is this? The difference, as always, lies in the differing functions and audiences. The marketing task, for example, draws on one's skills of organizing information into a coherent idea

PROJECT MEETING

Date: March 4

Attending: General Contractor, Owner, Architect, Mechanical Engineer

Construction Update:
- Installation of curtainwall is ongoing.
- Masonry to be completed in two weeks.
- Drywall installation begun in west wing, March 11.
- Ductwork in east wing to be finished in one week.
- Sprinkler system installed on first floor. Second floor to be finished in two weeks.

Stage of Completion:
- Structural Frame: 100%
- Roofing: 100%
- Exterior walls: 90%
- Doors and windows: 65%
- Mechanical: 50%
- Electrical wiring: 10%
- Sanitary Plumbing rough-in: 100%

Schedule:
  All work is on schedule.
  Finishes installation begins April 1.

Discussion:

Ceiling height in Classroom A and offices 10, 11 & 12 is low due to ductwork.
  Next month's meeting time needs to be rescheduled.
  Pricing on Change Order #3.

Actions items:

Mechanical Engineer to review calcs and discuss with subcontractor.

Meeting adjourned.

FIGURE 6.5 Meeting notes

or theme whereas meeting notes do not benefit from theming. They consist in recording discreet, only loosely related packets of information. They need to be comprehensive as well as continuous with prior and subsequent meeting notes to aid all parties in maintaining a clear sense of the project's current status and its progress toward completion. The tone should be blandly factual, regardless of the heat of disagreement that might have been generated at points in the meeting. Though it might make a juicy story back at the office if one of the participants became furious at some point, for the purpose of the meeting notes, it is an irrelevant event as long as it didn't result in a fist through a wall requiring a change order. Only then do you have an action item: "Contractor to repair fresh drywall hole 6″ in diameter and 42″ above the floor."

Field Reports

Part of an architect's job, oftentimes a precursor to a design commission, is to engage in a type of reconnaissance called a Field Report. Field Reports can serve numerous uses. To name a few

- Building owners often have need for a qualified professional to evaluate the aptness of an existing building for a new use.
- The important maintenance required to stabilize a deteriorating building needs to be identified.
- Applications for historic tax credits require extensive description of the building's historic elements.
- Rezoning applications may require a written evaluation of the existing surrounding buildings.
- A forensic report on the extent and cause of a building failure may be needed.

Through the Field Report, a potential client will often begin to develop an opinion about an architect's abilities through her facility with the written word long before she has the opportunity to form a judgment about the architect's worth as a designer. Thus, writing the field report requires as much care as preparing one's marketing materials.

The essence of a field report is this: observations are condensed and organized into a narrative description which becomes the basis for making recommendations, developing a strategy, or charting a course of action. Thus, to achieve a positive early impression by owners, regulators, and allied professionals, the ability to write a concise building description is essential. Field reports aim to be persuasive, but unlike marketing materials, which are asking potential clients to engage in a leap of faith, they do not attempt to do so by reaching emotional motivators. The field report is persuasive in the way that a scientist or art historian can be persuasive: by instilling confidence in the reader that the author has an authoritative grasp of the subject.

The conclusions of a field report should follow as the *logical consequences* of the exposition. For architects, this authoritative tone requires, to begin with, mastery of the precise technical terms with which to refer to parts of buildings. Nothing undermines the reader's presumption of the author's competence more quickly than the realization that she does not have command of the basic vocabulary of her trade. You should know, for example, that pilasters are not random bulges in a façade, that dormers are not merely roof windows, that cement is the chalky stuff in bags and concrete is what is delivered in a large truck, what the different basic patterns of brickwork are, the kinds of arches, what a wainscot is, the difference between a gutter and a downspout, and so on. Chapter 3 lists several available books of architectural terms. At least one should be with your ready-at-hand desk references.

The reason that mastery over a basic vocabulary of buildings instills confidence in the author is that it also determines what you can observe and say about buildings. For example, imagine how cumbersome it would be if, instead of using the word "footing," the author had to use the phrase "the part of the floor around the perimeter that turns down into the earth." The awkward wording that results would be bad enough, but the damage is greater than that. Not knowing that what one is looking at is called a "footing" means that the author is not even able to recognize the function a footing serves to spread the load from the slab and the walls into the earth at a bearing capacity the earth can support without sinking.

This is the real importance of a good vocabulary: it is the horizon of one's observations and thoughts.

Describing a building façade in a field report may seem like a simple task, but quite a lot has to come together to make the description logical and economical enough to enable the reader to develop a mental image. In what follows, a poor description of the Edmon Low Library building on the Oklahoma State University campus (Figure 6.6) will be improved for greater clarity, step-by-step until it is ready to be included in a report on the façade's overall condition and weathering.

> The South façade of the library building is a rectangle made of brick. It is three stories tall. A fourth story appears in dormers on the roof. Looking from left to right, there is a wing with a row of six windows, then a central piece with three brick

FIGURE 6.6 Edmon Low Library South Façade

arches that are round, then a right wing also with a row of six windows. Above the arches is a tower with brick at the base and a wooden lantern on top. On top of the tower is a dome. Each window on the left and right wings is a two-story high window on the first and second floor with a square window above at the third floor. As already mentioned, above each third floor window is a dormer for the fourth floor. There are three doorways in the arches. Above the doors is more glass. The columns separating the arches are Corinthian.

The author senses that a good way to organize a building description is from the general to the specific, but has trouble sticking to that plan. To begin with, to say that the building is a rectangle, even if the author is referring to the footprint and not the façade, is a misnomer. A rectangle is a specific abstract geometric shape. The plan or façade may well be *rectangular*, but it is never a *rectangle*. The second problem with the initial sentence is that it is a wasted opportunity to convey a broad-brush impression of the building if one neglects to mention its style. To say of a building that it is modernist, neo-Gothic, or in this case, Collegiate Georgian is to convey a great deal of information about the building's overall countenance, its emotional tone, and its employ of materials all in one or two words. Mention a style and a mental image quickly takes form. This opening sentence would also improve if some sense of the overall size were conveyed. If only by pacing it off, the author should be able to give a rough length. Mentioning that the façade is three stories tall already gives the reader a general idea of the height. All of this should occur in the first sentence, which can stand to become fairly dense with information.

> The South façade of the Edmon Low Library building is a brick-and-limestone Collegiate Georgian style composition approximately 200 feet long and three stories tall.

The first change made to this sentence is replacing the generic phrase "library building" with its full name. This is done in the name of improved specificity. Specificity and clarity are always closely related concepts. Next, descriptors are added leading up to the noun "composition." The word "limestone" is added because it is obviously a second major material on the façade neglected in the original description. Mentioning the architectural style early on in a description is always a good strategy. A style sums up so many material and form-making moves by an architect that its employ in an opening sentence does more than any other phrase can possibly do to help summon a mental image. Neglecting to mention the style is like going to the grocery store and coming home without the milk. It's that essential. Finally, after pacing the building, the author was able to estimate its length to be approximately 200 feet. This is essential if a mental image is to materialize. But this sentence can be further tightened up to the following:

> The brick-and-limestone Collegiate Georgian style south façade of the Edmon Low Library building is approximately 200 feet long and three stories tall.

Note that all the descriptors have been loaded into the sentence in advance of the anticipated subject. In the earlier sentence, the duty of serving as subject was split between "library" and "composition." Now they've been tightened into one. It is almost impossible to overload a noun with descriptors placed to the fore like this. Two sentences have been condensed into one and considerably more information has been conveyed. Indeed, the reader should be able to already form a general mental image. The remainder of the paragraph will just be a matter of filling in the details. A possible misconception must be cleared up, however, in the second sentence. The reader would at this point assume that the building is three stories tall when actually a fourth story is concealed in the roof. So it is essential that the next sentence clears up this possible misconception.

> A fourth story, indicated by dormers partially concealed by a parapet, is within the gabled roof.

Thus a possible misconception is both avoided and explained while at the same time, a more concise explanation of the roof form is introduced.

In sentence three ("Looking from left to right. . .") the author is attempting to deal with the disposition of façade elements such as windows, doors, arches, and columns, but, to do so, has introduced an undesirable element of subjectivity into what should be an objective description. In other words, suddenly someone standing and doing the looking has been unnecessarily introduced into what can and should be a purely objective description. Furthermore, in symmetrical façades, such as this one, it makes considerably more descriptive sense to begin in the middle and work one's way outward because this is actually how such buildings are conceived. So this sentence needs considerable reworking. The author needs to convey a sense of the major compositional elements on the façade, but how to do this in one sentence? He could say:

> The façade is divided into three parts, a central porch and wings on either side.

Thus making the "three parts" the subject of the sentence before launching into discussing the window and arches. But are the "three parts" really the most important thing to draw the reader's attention to, or are they, instead, descriptors of something else? When you look at the photo, what jumps out? The three tall brick arches dominate and organize—everything else in the façade composition is subordinate to them.

> The façade is symmetrical about a front porch consisting of three, full-height, brick entry arches infilled with glass and supporting a tower.

Thus, by stating that the façade is symmetrical about the brick arches, a three-part composition is implied and, therefore, doesn't even need to be expressly written. In keeping with the principle that it's almost impossible to load too many modifiers in front of a noun, the facts that the arches are made of brick and rise to the full height of the façade are mentioned. Since arches are inherently open forms, mentioning next what is underneath them follows naturally. Finally, introducing the subject of the tower leads easily into discussing the tower in more detail in the next sentence.

Unless the tower is to be the central subject of the report, judicious editing must be employed here since it is such a highly detailed and complex object. The basic materials and outline will suffice. First of all, though, a problem with terminology must be cleared-up: the dome-shaped structure at the top of the tower is a cupola, a small dome-topped structure for letting in light, as opposed to a dome, which in architecture is generally understood to be large enough to inhabit. So cupola it is. Since the tower consists of several distinct parts faced in different materials, it is not possible here to load all the modifiers ahead of a single subject.

> The tower consists of a rectangular brick base, a white wooden lantern and cupola.

Having addressed the overall shape and countenance of the building in the first sentence, cleared up a possible misconception that might have arisen out of the first sentence in the second sentence, and discussed the basic compositional parts in the third and the tower in the fourth, the paragraph is set to conclude with a discussion of the elements that exist at a finer level of detail (windows and pilasters) that are the last remaining character-giving elements to discuss. Since it has already been established that the façade is symmetrical, the implication is that the west side of the façade is identical to the east. Therefore, in the interest of brevity, the description should include both at once. Note that the next sentence opens with "As mentioned previously . . . ." This is always awkward and betrays poor organization of the description. It tells the reader that the description is so poorly assembled that the author must now backtrack. So the first thing to do is eliminate this source of awkwardness while still retaining the understanding that the pattern of the dormers follows that of the windows in the brick façade. What the author needs to convey here is the idea that each wing alternates six glazed window panels with five brick columns. This window pattern is contained at each end by large solid brick panels. But we can't say a "row of six windows" because a row implies horizontal alignment, and while the word "column" implies vertical alignment on a spreadsheet, the word has a precise meaning in architecture that would be confusing if employed here, as in "a column of windows." "Vertical row" just sounds like an oxymoron. This task is always a potential descriptive problem. If the glazing spans an entire structural bay, from one column to the next, it would be appropriate to say "six bays of glass" but there is no reason to think that each glass panel in this instance spans an entire bay. In fact, it probably does not. Even if it were a panel, it is not made of glass top-to-bottom anyway, but is defined by two-stories of glass curtainwall, above which is a square punched window and aligned above the punched window in the roof are the dormers. Ultimately, then, the two-story curtainwall section must be described first (as it is the most prominent). Then the punched windows can be mentioned along with the dormers.

> On each side of the porch, six, two-story high glass curtainwall panels separated by brick piers and flanked by solid brick panels are aligned with square punched windows at the third floor and with the dormers.

Note that the appropriate phrase here is "glass curtainwall" and not merely "curtainwall" as a curtainwall, while it is assumed is framed in metal, can have almost anything in the panels: stone, metal, wood, stucco, and glass. Finally, the last sentence in the original description can be deleted entirely. Even though it is a fact that the columns have Corinthian capitals, their existence is so insignificant to the composition that to include them here adds little to the desired mental picture.

Finally, the reconstructed description:

> The brick-and-limestone Collegiate Georgian style south façade of the Edmon Low Library building is approximately 200 feet long and three stories tall. A fourth story, indicated by dormers partially concealed by a parapet, is within the gabled roof. The façade is symmetrical about a front porch consisting of three, full-height, brick entry arches infilled with glass and supporting a tower. The tower consists of a rectangular brick base, a white wooden lantern and cupola. On each side of the porch,

six, two-story high glass curtainwall panels separated by brick piers and flanked by solid brick panels are aligned with square punched windows at the third floor and with the dormers.

Ten sentences in the original description have been cut in half, yet more detailed information is conveyed. Most importantly, the description follows logically from general to specific elements enabling a mental image to materialize in stages of specificity. Though this analysis of one façade description has been lengthy, it contains lessons that apply to many of the common mistakes made in trying to achieve clarity and objectivity in recording one's observations.

Your skill at writing field reports, meeting notes, specifications, proposals, and marketing materials should be practiced before attempting the real thing for others. Although architects, of course, wish to be judged primarily on the quality of their design skills, the business and technical writing architects do is an important source of first impression of their intelligence and professionalism. Furthermore, the clarity with which these writing tasks are accomplished is an important safeguard for realizing the highest possible design quality. Thus, the skill with which you compose your marketing materials, proposals, and technical writing stands to be either a vehicle to help realize your design aspirations, or for those who treat these tasks carelessly and neglectfully, a hindrance to overcome.

As you advance in a firm from intern to project architect to management, skill at business writing becomes increasingly valued. Indeed, the confidence with which owners and managers perceive they can allow you to represent the firm in writing stands to either help or hinder your upward mobility. Though the genres of business writing differ, and therefore the rhetorical standards also vary, they all have in common the need to communicate with an external audience. Whether the writing task is authoring a cover letter, marketing materials, or the writing necessary to shepherd a project through to completion, the key to successful business writing is to merge brevity with clarity appropriate to the task.

1. Go on the internet and download three firms' mission statements you find to be particularly well expressed and one that you find to be poorly written. Be prepared to present them and discuss your reasons. Then write your own.

2. Write descriptions of three of your projects. Then write an overall statement explaining what unites them and what makes them unique.

3. Describe a building façade for a field report, then give the description to a friend or classmate to see if he or she can draw the façade based on the written description.

exercises

STATEMENTS OF DESIGN PHILOSOPHY AND MANIFESTOS

As you finish school and move into the profession, you will find that you need to be able to explain your design philosophy or outlook—to potential employers, on graduate school applications, to explain professional activities to the public, and to potential clients, all who deserve to know if your values are a good match for theirs. But, perhaps most importantly, you have come to a point in your career where you need to clarify what you believe and the values you hold to yourself. Mastering the two related writing activities presented in this chapter, the design statement and the manifesto, will help prepare you for these occasions. The design statement and the manifesto are related in that they both are a declaration of self and where you stand in relation to architecture —that is, they both get at your core values. They do differ, however, in their scope: a design philosophy is a statement that tells the reader what values you wish your work to represent and why you hold these concepts. A manifesto goes further to express a larger validity that is designed to actually pull your audience along with you, convincing the reader of a lack in current architectural thought and how you propose to rectify the situation. It is a sustained argument born of dissatisfaction with the current state of thought in architecture. We will get into more detail about both genres as the chapter progresses.

A STATEMENT OF DESIGN PHILOSOPHY

A statement of design philosophy must be succinct: typically a short one-page piece that summarizes your core values about design. This piece may be viewed by either the internal or the external discourse community. That is, you are simply making a statement that says, "Here I stand and this is why." When we talk about manifestos later, you will see that manifestos are designed to be read and engaged by the internal discourse community and that the burden on you as a writer in that situation is to express a larger validity than just your own. For now, with the design statement, you will stick to your own reality.

On the surface, it may seem that writing one page about yourself would be a fairly easy task. However, condensing four or more years of architecture and design experience, knowledge, and feelings is not an easy task. You will want to try to say it all, but you can't. So, the task is to choose the material that represents what it is most important for you to say about yourself. This brings us to a second point about writing your design statement: you will be working with abstract concepts, but your readers will not be able to grasp your unique perspective on the abstract unless you anchor them in concrete material. So there are two challenges to writing a statement of your design philosophy:

1. Compressing your experience.
2. Concretizing your experience.

The first places a premium on the ability to summarize, the second on creating details and supporting materials that help the reader enter your experience through thoughts, feelings or physical descriptions.

To begin, you will want to collect the material from which you will build your statement. This will be substantial. You will want to go all the way back to your first year. Your design journal (see Chapter 2) will be very helpful in this process. By examining your reflections over the years, you will be able to see patterns of feeling and thinking and especially how they have evolved. Just as in a novel or a play, the lead character must have a story arc, so in the story of the development and evolution of your design sensibility over the years there should be an arc. Your arc is to explain how and why your values or attitudes have changed over time. In examining your design projects, you will be able to identify developments in your skills through your design experiences. Going over course notes will help you find the occasional quote or note about a particular architect that influenced your thinking. Digging through your travel sketches and photographs will remind you of the experiences with design that may have surprised you or held you in awe. These are the materials from which your core values will emerge. We recommend that you spend quite a bit of time with these materials. You may want to write observations or reflections about some of them in your design notebook to help you think about what each might offer your design statement. Remember, you are summarizing your experience, which means you are taking the most formative aspects and articulating them for your audience.

Those materials you sift through and examine for meaning will also help you address the second task: concretizing your values. That is, the quote, event, travel story, photo, sketch, or building that you have unearthed may provide the concrete anchor for an abstract concept you think represents your core values. This can be tricky. For example, the following simple identity statement may at first glance seem concrete enough:

Architecture is art.

However, the statement is so general that the reader has no idea what about architecture (a complex multi-layered phenomenon) could be art and what about art (a huge category) could be architecture. What kind of architecture? What in architecture is art? What kind of art—movement? painting? sculpture? etc.

Better is the following (Figure 7.1):

> Architecture is a puzzle; there are many pieces that fit
> together to form the whole. And when all the pieces—
> Reason, Context, Response—are combined in the correct
> mixture, a building comes to life.[1]

In this case, the student has given the reader a concrete image within which the more general concept of architecture can be understood. It also allows her to map the concept of puzzle pieces to more abstract concepts of "reason, context and response" in a way that helps the reader understand the concept of architecture's important constituent elements. This kind of metaphorical mapping can be an effective way to organize a design statement.

As a rule of thumb, you will want to anchor each abstract statement you make with a detailed example or explanation to ground each paragraph. See the following student paragraph for an example of explaining an abstract concept.

> I am an architect, a designer who seeks to stand in the gap
> for others. I use my skill to push for a better future. I believe
> that to create Architecture one must look at the past to move
> forward into the future—to reclaim and reuse things once
> created. Reclamation is an important part of creating the
> ultimate sustainable environment.[2]

This student goes on to explain that to "stand in the gap for others" means to create a better future through architecture and more specifically through reclamation in order to achieve sustainability. Notice how she builds this throughout the paragraph.

While it may be tempting to move from one concept to the next as you move through the paragraphs of your design philosophy, your vision will be better served if you limit the number of concepts that you apply to your vision. This will create a more powerful statement for your reader.

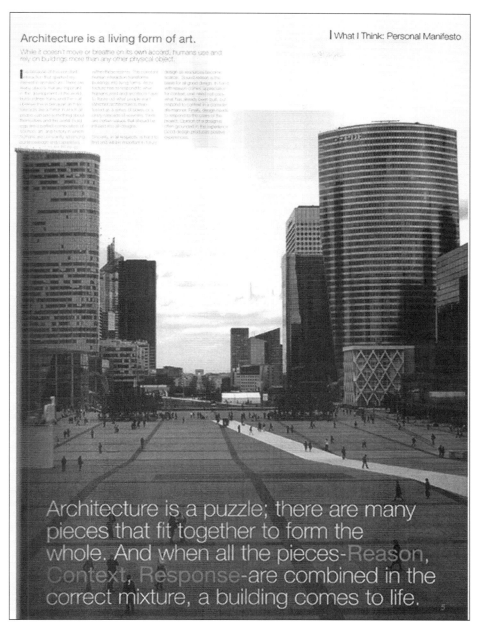

FIGURE 7.1 Combining words and images in a Statement of Design Philosophy

Here are other questions that may help you define your design position:

- What is your design process? Has it developed over time? Why and how?
- What role does history play for you? Is there a particular architectural period that speaks to you more than others?
- Is there a certain architect's work that you admire? Why?
- What reading, travel or other personal experience influences your view of design/architecture?
- Is there a particular style you admire? What is it that draws you to that style? Have you developed your own style? If so, how and on what basis has this development taken place?

You may want to do some journal entries that specifically answer these questions. Unlike the other types of writing covered in earlier chapters, the material for this writing project comes from the self. Reflection, as we discussed in Chapter 2, is a way to have a conversation. In this situation, the conversation is between you and your thoughts and design processes. This includes reflecting on why certain design ideas were successful and some were not—the stages at which your design thinking was affirmed or you had to find a new way of approaching a design problem. It also includes your reactions to architectural concepts; for example, you may have had difficulty with a concept or resistance to an architect's position or rejected a particular design. Why?

Now is the time for you to find the common patterns of thinking, common threads of outlook or bias, and times when something engaged your imagination or surprised you. This entails more than just a passing relationship with the material you will be reviewing to include in your paper. Once you have clarified your position, it is time to articulate it.

Here is how an architect seized on one aspect of his thinking to guide a personal statement of his design philosophy:

Much is said these days about how architecture should respect nature, how it should embrace natural processes, and be a force for healing between mankind and nature. But what stands out for me about architecture is how it *endures,* and an important measure of its success is how well it *resists* the forces of nature; how well it ages. The quality of durability is precisely the one magazines and photos are least able to capture, but is one humans are immediately able to sense in actual encounters.

No matter how sensitively attuned to nature a building's design is, we should never forget that it is still an intervention in the natural scheme of things. No doubt nature will eventually triumph, but my job is to forestall that eventuality for as long as possible. This cause is best served by designing buildings that are well-made, using quality materials, and by making them both useful and beautiful so that humans (the ultimate wild-card in nature's plan) will want to help stave-off the inevitable. This is my bid for immortality.

Here we can see the work of compressing and concretizing brought together in a single passage. In the first paragraph the author selects and then compresses one important aspect of his thinking. He begins by establishing an element of his thought that departs from what he sees as the prevailing wisdom. He then suggests a reason why something he thinks important is neglected by others. This is his opening to stating what is unique about his approach. The second paragraph concretizes the thought established in the first paragraph by explaining his strategy for putting it into action. Note that the passage does not even try to summarize a designer's whole existence. It takes one idea held dear and expands on its larger implications to make it an encompassing thought.

THE MANIFESTO

The word "Manifesto" has an old-fashioned sound to it, but manifestos have played an important role in architecture's development and progress. Let's start with a definition of "manifesto." The Oxford English Dictionary has these definitions:

1. a. A public declaration or proclamation, written or spoken; *esp.* a printed declaration, explanation, or justification of policy issued by a head of state, government, or political party or candidate, or any other individual or body of individuals of public relevance, as a school or movement in the Arts.

b. In extended use: a book or other work by a private individual supporting a cause, propounding a theory or argument, or promoting a certain lifestyle.

2. A proof, a piece of evidence.[3]

In a manifesto, you will be making a public declaration that will promote your own perspective of architecture with proof. You will be expected to provide the "why" rather than the "how" of what you find most important philosophically in your experience of architecture.

In architecture, manifestos have played the role of theory building. Le Corbusier's *Toward a New Architecture* in 1923 and Robert Venturi's *Complexity and Contradiction in Architecture* in 1966 were seminal works in shifting architectural thought toward Modernism and Post-Modernism respectively. See the opening to Le Corbusier's book, which constitutes his manifesto:

In every field of industry, new problems have presented themselves and new tools have been created capable of resolving them. If this new fact be set against the past, then you have revolution.

In building and construction, mass-production had already been begun; in face of new economic needs, mass-production units have been created both in mass and detail, and definite results have been achieved both in detail and in mass.

If this fact be set against the past, then you have revolution, both in the method employed and in the large scale on which it has been carried out.

The history of Architecture unfolds itself slowly across the centuries as a modification of structure and ornament, but in the last fifty years steel and concrete have brought new conquests, which are the index of a greater capacity for construction, and of an architecture in which the old codes have been overturned. If we challenge the past, we shall learn that "styles" no longer exist for us, that a style belonging to our own period has come about; and there has been a revolution.

Our minds have consciously or unconsciously apprehended these events and new needs have arisen, consciously or unconsciously. The machinery of Society, profoundly *out of gear*, oscillates between an amelioration, of historical importance, and a catastrophe.

The primordial instinct of every human being is to assure himself of a shelter.

The various classes of workers in society to-day *no longer have dwellings adapted to their needs; neither the artisan nor the intellectual.*

It is a question of building which is at the root of the social unrest of to-day; architecture or revolution.[4]

This famous manifesto draws on the social issues of the times and connects the conditions of the built environment, i.e. the consequences for architecture of mass production and the development of materials such as concrete and steel, to set up his call to architecture (Figure 7.2). The paragraphs follow a thread of logic even though it is not marked with the usual transitions such as "therefore" or "hence." Notice his use of "revolution" throughout —in paragraph one "then you have revolution," then in paragraph three "then you have revolution," and again in paragraph four where he introduces Architecture into the picture he says "there has been a revolution." He sets up the fact that the revolution has already taken place and proposes architecture as the next step for shelter is the basic instinct of mankind, but the current buildings do not serve the purpose of any class of human. He powerfully delivers the punch at the very end of the manifesto—will we choose architecture (which is the answer to the current human dilemma) or revolution (already happened). Notice the use of "we" and "our" in this piece: Le Corbusier is drawing the reader in with this use of the first person pronouns.

FIGURE 7.2 Grain elevators inspired Le Corbusier's famous Manifesto, *Towards a New Architecture*

This piece of writing persuasiveness derives from its strong images and ideas; drawing on the reader's background knowledge of the social, architectural, and industrial; and from its logical form using repetition and simple sentence structure to reinforce the powerful ideas. Written forty years later, Robert Venturi's "gentle manifesto" is as powerful as Le Corbusier, but crafted to his times and the issues that he is drawing attention to:

> I like complexity and contradiction in architecture. I do not like the incoherence or arbitrariness of incompetent architecture nor the precious intricacies of picturesqueness or expressionism. Instead, I speak of a complex and contradictory architecture based on the richness and ambiguity of modern experience, including that experience which is inherent in art. Everywhere, except in architecture, complexity and contradiction have been acknowledged, from Godel's proof of ultimate inconsistency in mathematics to T.S. Eliot's analysis of "difficult" poetry and Joseph Albers' definition of the paradoxical quality of painting.
>
> But architecture is necessarily complex and contradictory in its very inclusion of the traditional Vitruvian elements of commodity, firmness, and delight. And today the wants of program, structure, and mechanical equipment, and expression, even in single buildings in simple contexts, are diverse and conflicting in ways previously unimaginable. The increasing dimension and scale of architecture in urban and regional planning add to the difficulties. I welcome the problems and exploit the uncertainties. By embracing contradiction as well as complexity, I aim for vitality as well as validity.
>
> Architects can no longer afford to be intimidated by the puritanically moral language of orthodox Modern architecture. I like elements which are hybrid rather than "pure," compromising rather than "clean," distorted rather than "straightforward," ambiguous rather than "articulated," perverse as well as impersonal, boring as well as "interesting," conventional as well as "designed," accommodating rather than excluding, redundant rather

than simple, vestigial as well as innovating, inconsistent and equivocal rather than direct and clear. I am for messy vitality over obvious unity. I include the nonsequitur [sic] and proclaim the duality.

I am for richness of meaning rather than clarity of meaning; for the implicit function as well as the explicit function. I prefer "both-and" to "either-or," black and white and sometimes gray, to black or white, and sometimes gray, to black or white. A valid architecture evokes many levels of meaning and combinations of focus; its space and its elements become readable and workable in several ways at once.

But an architecture of complexity and contradiction has a special obligation toward the whole; its truth must be in its totality or its implications of totality. It must embody the difficult unity of inclusion rather than the easy unity of exclusion. More is not less.[5]

In a manifesto, the writing should emulate what is being argued; that is, there is a distinctly artistic element (requirement) to the manifesto. For example, Le Corbusier's argument for modernism is a piece of writing that is itself distinctly modernistic, dispensing with much of the usual ornament of writing and using high-impact verbs. Venturi's "gentle manifesto," however, adopts a tone that instantiates his rejection of the absolutism he finds so objectionable in modernism. He begins, "I like complexity and contradiction in architecture" thereby softening by personalizing the argument as against Le Corbusier's severely objective tone. This artistic requirement of the manifesto is, as we shall see later, brilliantly exploited by Rem Koolhaas in his essay "Junkspace." If you are writing to promote the beauty of economy, then your writing should be similarly economical. If you seek to promote inclusiveness, then your writing should be plain spoken. If instead, you seek to exalt architecture as an art form, then the sky's the limit with the complexity of the writing. We recommend that you read Venturi's in the same way we have "read" Le Corbusier's. These giants of architecture provide a standard for which to strive as you write your own manifesto.

Writing a manifesto will be your opportunity to connect theory and practice in thoughtful ways based on your own experience and reflection. Manifestos are a synthesis of architectural concepts, your knowledge of history, design experience and your personal perspective. It is a version of finding your voice as a writer.

GETTING STARTED

First of all, you need to know your design position, but it will not magically appear for you. This will require some thought and perhaps reflection. You may want to start with how your thoughts about architecture have changed since you started your architecture program. To help with this process, go back to your journals, course notes, and design projects to help you decide what position to take in your manifesto. What has troubled or challenged you about architecture? Its creation? Its public reception, the conditions of practice, the culture that surrounds its production, its place in society? Now is the occasion to branch-out from the internal disciplinary knowledge of architecture and engage ALL you've learned in school. Bring in ecology, psychology, politics, economics, sociology, art, philosophy, and current events to help form and bolster an argument. Be willing to engage the big questions: Why ARE so many people homeless in Western nations? IS this an architectural problem? What CAN architects realistically do about global warming? Why ARE the suburbs so ugly? And what is beauty anyway? What IS to be done about the loss of place? Why ARE architects so often powerless? It is a long list, limited only by your horizons.

DEVELOPING YOUR DESIGN POSITION

A manifesto is first and foremost an attempt to persuade. It is your opportunity to use the power of language to persuade other architects to your point. And it is a way to become known, as Charles Jencks asserts:

These are directed at other architects, to hypnotise them. The general public would stop reading—but that does not deter the polemicist, who is looking to tantalise a sect. To read a polemic, you have to want the expected outcome since the manifesto is made more to keep an audience united than to convert the heathen.[6]

Jencks may have overstated his case here; manifestos also seek to convince the undecided. Polemic is an extreme kind of controversial argument. You will want to think of how this argument will affect this insider audience. You want to have an effect that will not just engage the intellectual side of the architecture community, but its heart as well. You will want to be passionate in your persuasion. It is therefore essential that you remember why you are writing the manifesto. It is also important to remember that a manifesto is where you simultaneously make "manifest" yourself but at the same time build community. This may seem contradictory: you are articulating a very personal perspective, but you are doing so to create a change or extension in thinking of the architectural community: "There is one more important aspect to the genre: the personal element . . .The most effective manifestos, such as Le Corbusier's *Toward a New Architecture* (1923) constantly address the reader as 'you' and reiterates the joint 'we' until an implied pact is built up between author and convert. A manifesto must manifest itself to you, personally."[7]

The seeming paradoxes of the manifesto do not end there. One might think that engaging a community would require mild, conventional approaches to expressing one's position. For example, when we discussed writing architecture history in Chapter 3, we talked about sticking with the structure and the conventions of argument-making in order to engage the audience. However, manifestos by their very nature are inflammatory, contradictory, and challenging to the very audience they are pitched. Jencks encapsulates this, "The good manifesto mixes a bit of terror, runaway emotion and charisma with a lot of common sense."[8]

In addition, conventional means of getting the message across are counter to the goal of manifest-making and as such, "use any rhetorical tools available—rhymes, bad jokes, puns, outrageous untruths . . . and they always mint new metaphors."[9]

Consider this excerpt from the introduction to Rem Koolhaas' piece "Junkspace":

> If space-junk is the human debris that litters the universe, junkspace is the residue mankind leaves on the planet. The . . . product of modernization is not modern architecture but Junkspace. Junkspace is what remains after modernization has run its course or, more precisely, what coagulates while modernization is taking place, its fall-out . . .
>
> More and more, more is more. Junkspace is overripe and undernourishing at the same time, a colossal security blanket that covers the earth, the sum of all decisions not taken, issues not faced, choices not made, priorities left undefined . . . corruption tolerated . . . Junkspace is like being condemned to a perpetual Jacuzzi with millions of your best friends.[10]

Koolhaas has coined the new term "junkspace" to symbolize the central theme of his piece. He has taken on the concept of modernization and is using "junkspace" as a way of talking about where architecture fits in the process of modernization (Figure 7.3).

FIGURE 7.3 Junkspace

And he does so in an energetic flood of words meant to replicate the state of affairs he is describing. So, as you think about staking your position, use your imagination to connect your claims with the way you express them.

The manifesto should be memorable, in that it should stay in the mind of the reader sometimes as a thorn or uncomfortable litany. In fact, Jencks suggests that the manifesto often resembles:

first grade recitation, responses in church:

- Post-Modern is a paradox—After, Now, Post-Present
- Post-Modern is 'posteriority', after all time
- Post-Modern is the desire to live outside, beyond, after
- Post-Modern is the time-binding of past, present, future
- Post-Modern is the continuation of Modernism and its transcendence.[11]

Jenks calls us to notice that these are memorable lines that could be set to music.

Consider, for example, the following lines from Louis I. Kahn's "Order is":

Design is form-making in order
Form emerges out of a system of construction
Growth is a construction
In **order** is creative force
In **design** is the means—where with what when with
    how much

. . .

Through the **nature**—why
Through the **order**—what
Through **design**—how[12]

Though these triplets are taken from different parts of the piece, notice how Kahn used repetition and bolding to create a memorable text. The audience not only gets a sense of how these concepts fit together through language, but also the visual placement of the text as we will see later in the chapter.

You want to be memorable in your declaration of self. As these examples illustrate, there are various ways to accomplish this through the process of creating, organizing, and articulating your design position. Part of what makes a manifesto memorable is its consistent emotional tone achieved through language. With Le Corbusier, the tone is impatience for the coming revolution. Venturi wants us to be more reflective. Koolhaas is caustic with sarcasm and irony. Kahn adopts the tone of the wise teacher. In each case, consistency is the key. We will discuss the ways you can use language to better reflect your thinking later in the chapter.

CREATING A MANIFESTO

Unlike other types of writing, which have fairly specific expectations for structure, manifestos are presented in various forms, reflective of the writer and the unique architectural position. A caution is required here, however. Although there is more flexibility in writing manifestos, you must remember that the audience still needs to be engaged with the text. You don't want to get so creative that the audience cannot discern your main position or the support for that position. If the audience cannot make any sense of what you are writing, it will give up completely on trying to understand the point you are aiming to make. Making the connections for the reader is of utmost importance for a successful paper.

Let's look at an example of a manifesto, which takes its energy from Vitruvius' concepts of *utilitas, firmitas*, and *venustas*. We have provided two drafts of this manifesto to show how you can take ideas and make them more effective.

First Draft

It has been said since the time of Vitruvius that architecture creates utilitas, firmitas and venustas.

It's also been called commodity, firmness and delight. A modern restatement: functionality, durability and art. Does architecture create these qualities or require them?

But none of this is possible without sustainability.

When it uses up too much land, contributes to global warming, uses too many resources, makes people less equal, is made only to make more money, doesn't know why it exists, becomes out-of-date, and ignores the important things in life, then it cannot be sustainable.

Only if it's sustainable does architecture function, endure, and become beautiful.

Sustainability is not a LEED certification. It is not a style or a look. A concern for sustainability will never be sugarcoating for a bitter pill for me. It will always be my starting point, an outlook, a way of life.

Observe first the arrangement of the text: it is clumped together so that key words are buried within the text. The first sentence starts with an empty subject—"It" does not refer to a specific entity. The reader has to wait until the end of the sentence to find some important words. Ideas are thrown in without a sense of development of a central theme here. There is the question "Does architecture create these qualities or require them?" but what follows cannot be construed as some kind of response. Now read a revised version.

Revised

Vitruvius told us that architecture creates *utilitas, firmitas* and *venustas.*

Or is that commodity, firmness and delight?

Or should we say, today: functionality, durability and art?

And should we ask: Does it create these qualities or demand them?

But how is any of this possible without being sustainable?

Architecture which devours the landscape, heats the planet, consumes too much, increases inequality, serves only the bottom line, loses its purpose, becomes quickly obsolete, and forgets that what is important cannot be sustainable. LEED certification does not guarantee sustainability. Neither does a certain look.

Instead, it depends on how you begin. A concern for architecture's sustainability will always be my starting point. It will never be a sugar-coating for a bitter pill.

Only that which is sustainable can meet its function over time.

Only that which is sustainable endures.

Only the sustainable is truly beautiful.

Notice how the manifesto starts with a sentence that has a full subject—and not only a full subject, but a subject that will be familiar to an architecture audience. Also, the terms *utilitas, firmitas,* and *venustas* have been italicized. This brings the readers' attention to their importance here. By invoking Vitruvius, the writer has grounded his manifesto in architecture. Notice the effective use of space and questions in this version. Notice also that the questions form the basis for what follows and that is the central notion that sustainability arises out of the fundamental questions of architecture. In this text, the questions provide a bridge between what is already known to the reader and what the writer wants the reader to know by the end. Notice also that the manifesto ends with a call that is evoked through repetition and strong language that ties it back to the fundamental concepts of *utilitas, firmitas,* and *venustas.* Similar to the statements from Jencks earlier, there is a rhythmic quality to the statements—a litany of "only" in this case.

MAKING AN ARGUMENT

In earlier chapters, we discussed how you respond when asked to make an argument about a building, a group of buildings, a particular architect's style or a period of architecture. Writing a manifesto makes an argument but from a reflective stance—the reflective stance is discussed in Chapter 2 on journals. Argument, in this case, means persuading your reader to think about your design position in a deep way. However, you need to be able to present your argument in a way in which the reader is invited to come to believe something new in the process. Doing this may require a different approach from that used in an academic paper or a work report. Your argument may seem less linear than other types of writing. The points of your argument may be punctuated by more dramatic or poetic examples than you are accustomed to using. The argument will be there, but much less explicit than you might see in other types of persuasive writing. Manifestos may, but do not necessarily, engage in strictly syllogistic presentation of ideas. Indeed, you may well be assembling ideas that ordinarily are not seen together. The argument, then, may consist in how skillfully the author inflames the emotions. Shame, status, hope, fear, desire, guilt, and love are all fair game.

ORGANIZING AND DEVELOPING A MANIFESTO

You will need to decide how to organize your manifesto. The organization should match the way you are approaching the topic. For example, if following a prose style, you will want to think about your organization much in the way we discussed in Chapter 3. Ask yourself what makes the most sense in terms of what you are trying to accomplish. In Chapter 3, we suggested that paragraphs could be arranged chronologically or spatially. When thinking about your design position or concept, what would make the most sense in designing your paragraph organization?

Notice the headings from the "Charter of the New Urbanism" organize the content of the charter from larger to smaller entities:

> We assert the following principles to guide public policy, development practice, urban planning, and design:
> The region: Metropolis, city and town
> . . .

The neighborhood, the district, and the corridor

. . .

The block, the street, and the building.[13]

However, if using an unconventional style, you need to find other ways to organize ideas. For example, you could use numbers or bulleted lists, italics, bold or configuration of text blocks that are unusual and visually striking. Notice the second half of Louis I. Kahn's "Order is" piece below:

Through the **nature**—why
Through the **order**—what
Through the **design**—how
A form emerges from the structural elements inherent in the form.

A dome is not conceived when questions arise how to build it.
Nervi grows an arch
Fuller grows a dome
Mozart's compositions are designs
They are exercises of order—intuitive
Design encourages more designs
Designs derive their imagery from order
Imagery is the memory—the form
Style is an adopted order
The same **order** created the elephant and created man
They are different designs
Begun from different aspirations
Shaped from different circumstances
Order does not imply Beauty
The same order created the dwarf and Adonis
Design is not making Beauty
Beauty emerges from selection
affinities
integration
love
Art is a form-making life in order—psychic

Order is intangible

> It is a level of creative consciousness
> forever becoming higher in level
> The higher the order the more diversity in design

Order supports integration

From what the space wants to be the unfamiliar may be revealed to the architect.

From order he will derive creative force and power of self-criticism to give form to this unfamiliar.

Beauty will evolve.[14]

Kahn provides us with a piece that is organized by the space the text occupies. The use of white space and text helps the reader "see" where the manifesto is going. The use of bold font also draws the reader's eye to the most important points of the text. You may want to consider this kind of spatial organization if it fits your design position. After all, you are an architect: think like one. That is to say, if this were a design project, how would you make the organization fit your manifesto's parti?

Another suggestion is to read manifestos to get ideas. Ulrich Conrad's *Programs and Manifestos on 20th-Century Architecture* and Kate Nesbitt's *Theorizing a New Agenda for Architecture* contain many examples.

Supporting material should relate to your design position because this will not always be evident to the reader. See how the following example does NOT help the reader understand the design position.

> Creating a sense of place is always important for the architect.
> The notions of *genius loci* helps us remember that.
> Memories are made.
> Guardians are near
> Finding the right place is important
> The unseen plays a role.
> It's all in the experience.

This example is a jumble of ideas—*memories, guardians, unseen, experience* that aren't connected with the design position of the *genius loci*. As a result, the reader is confused rather than convinced of anything. There are two places that this manifesto could use some work: first, in the introductory material, and, second, in the list. Let's look at a revised version:

> As architects, we are sensitive to how the users of a particular space will experience and then remember that place. Both seen and unseen elements contribute to the *genius loci*.
> A waft of perfume at the edge of a memory
> A final parting
> The spirit of place guarding myths of snake and dish
> In jealous contours
> Of order, form, love and beauty
> Seeing, hearing, smelling, touching tasting.
> In space
>
> *Genius loci* is the human experience of place.

INCLUDING VISUALS AS PART OF YOUR MANIFESTO

The manifesto assignment may allow you to include visuals— sketches, diagrams or other images. Again, because the manifesto is such a personal piece of writing, you will have opportunity to be imaginative with choices. However, don't forget that there is an audience, so your visual should communicate something, and have an effective design—after all, the audience values good design and you want to get and keep its attention. You may want to refer back to Chapter 3 where we discuss effectively integrating visuals with text.

DOCUMENTATION/PLAGIARISM/ INTERTEXTUALITY

Just a quick note about plagiarism here. While the manifesto is presumably a text generated from your own head, you may use some borrowed material. If that is the case, be sure that any borrowed material—visual or textual—that is not your own is documented properly.

LANGUAGE CONVENTIONS

In a manifesto, language is generally more pointed and terse and it is reflective of the voice of the individual writer.

Manifestos, because of the tendency for the writers to make declarations and to the need to be memorable contain *parallelism*. Parallelism is the use of the same grammatical form to show an equal relationship between ideas. One thing to keep in mind when doing parallel constructions is to keep words with words, phrases with phrases, and sentences with sentences. See the following example for a violation in parallelism in type of grammatical construction:

> Non-Parallel: architecture is order, always in a form, and design.

> Parallel: architecture is order, form, and design.

Replacing "always in a form" with the word "form" makes the items in the list parallel.

There are other, more complex ways where equal ideas are presented grammatically; for example, with a coordinating conjunction such as *and, but, yet*. Notice in the examples below, sentences labeled (a) are not parallel, but (b) are.

> (a) Positive space is *to dwell in*, but negative space is for moving.
> (b) Positive space is *for dwelling*, but negative space is for moving.

> (a) A *parti* is used to express an idea and *describing* the spatial hierarchy of a plan.
> (b) A *parti* is used to express an idea and *(to) describe* the spatial hierarchy of a plan.

> (a) John traveled to Italy in the summer to see the classic architecture but also *sketching* the buildings.
> (b) John traveled to Italy in the summer to see the classic architecture but also *to sketch* the buildings.

Consider the list of points that Deborah Berke makes in her headings in "Thoughts on the Everyday" in which she is creating a call for attention to the ordinary in an architecture of the everyday. In the first six points she makes (all followed by an explanation), she uses the repetition of "An Architecture of the Everyday May Be." "May be" is used rather than "is" because "an architecture of the everyday resists strict definition; any rigorous attempt at a concise delineation will inevitably lead to contradictions."[15] These are stated below:

> An Architecture of the Everyday May Be Generic and
> Anonymous.
> An Architecture of the Everyday May Be Banal or Common.
> An Architecture of the Everyday May Therefore Be Quite
> Ordinary.
> An Architecture of the Everyday May Be Crude.
> An Architecture of the Everyday May Be Sensual.
> An Architecture of the Everyday May Also Be Vulgar and
> Visceral.[16]

Then, in the next set of headings, "may be" is replaced by "may" plus a verb other than "be" or by a straight verb:

> Acknowledges Domestic Life.
> May Take on Collective and Symbolic Meaning but It Is Not
> Necessarily Monumental.
> Responds to Program and Is Functional.
> May Change as quickly as Fashion, but It Is Not Always
> Fashionable.[17]

The final line that concludes the series contains a definite *to be* verb "is." Berke is making a fact out of all of these "may be" statements. This is emphasized by the fact that there is no text that follows the statement.

> The Architecture of the Everyday is Built.[18]

So, you can see how the manifesto is subtly organized in a continuum by less and more definite grammatical forms, in this case, from "may be" which is very tentative to "is" which is very definite, to build the design position of this manifesto.

Recall that writing for a particular audience calls for not only specialized vocabulary choices but also sentence structure and language choices that send messages about the writer's position toward the ideas that she is writing about. In the case of manifestos, this entails using language for architects who are aware of the theories of architecture and of the manifestos that have shaped those theories. Remember also, as we stated at the beginning of the chapter, the manifesto is a declaration of your position that is meant to engage not just the minds of your audience members but also their passions. In this section, we will discuss ways you can use language to, as we indicated earlier, help you make yourself manifest.

Powerful and shorter forceful sentences are one way to effectively make this work.

> Long and rambling: In the order of things that architects do, we must consider the fact that *genius loci* as a sense of place is an important concept to attend to for all of us.

> Short and powerful: Pay attention to *genius loci*.

To establish the tone of your manifesto you will want to state opinions as facts. Active rather than passive sentences and appropriate verbs are specific ways you can achieve this.

There are times when the passive voice is appropriate and useful, but you will want to consider using it sparingly in your manifesto. See the following example of a sentence that is rendered in the passive and active voices:

> Passive: *Genius loci* is created through architecture.

> Active: Architecture creates *genius loci*.

How did you respond to those two sentences? Two things are important to think about when you shift from a passive to an active construction:

1. The sentence is shorter.
2. You are placing the actor of the sentence in a prominent position; thereby, giving her a more powerful placement.

Where you place the agent noun is a consideration here—to highlight *genius loci*, you may want to use the passive, but consider how the flow of the manifesto will read if you shift the actor to the end of a sentence.

We often tell student writers to use active verbs such as *run, create, throw, send* rather than stative verbs such as *is, are, does, has.* In the case of the manifesto, you are making declarations just as Kahn and Berke do:

> Growth is a construction.[19]
>
> Beauty will evolve.[20]
>
> The Architecture of the Everyday is Built.[21]

The stative verb in these cases performs an important function: it announces a moment of conclusion. It has isolated an important identity. When you consider your sentences for your manifesto, think about a good mix of active verbs and stative verbs.

You will also want to take into consideration your use of transitions between ideas as well as be aware of how you are signaling your information to the reader. In Chapter 3, we discussed the fact that in writing architecture history, you needed to consider that academics ground their credibility and arguments in language such as transition words of certainty balanced with qualifiers. In that way you don't overstate your position. However, when writing the manifesto, using cautious language will not serve your purpose. You will want to use language that is striking and bold. You may not use transitions at all deciding instead that highlighting or repeating certain words or juxtaposing words or phrases will do the work that transitions usually do.

A grammatical stumbling block that often undermines strong writing is the dangling or misplaced modifier. Dangling modifiers are either a single word or a phrase that refers to something in the sentence that is not there. For example,

> Dangling modifier: After finishing the first design class, the teamwork got easier.

The problem with the modifying phrase "after finishing the first design class" is that the person who did the finishing is not mentioned in the main clause "the teamwork got easier." The easiest way to correct dangling modifiers is to ask, "Who is doing the action in the dangling phrase and in the main clause." In this case, we could correct the dangling modifier by revising the main clause.

> Correct: After finishing the first design class, I found that the teamwork got easier.

Let's look at some other examples.

> Dangling modifier: While it doesn't have emotion, people see buildings as having human qualities.

In this case "it" does not appear as a subject in the main clause. So, this can be corrected as such:

> Correct: While they do not have emotions, buildings are often viewed as having human qualities.

Misplace modifiers occur when the modifying word or phrase is positioned away from what it refers to.

> Misplaced modifier: I sketched the Eiffel Tower when I was in Paris in watercolor.

In this case, "in watercolor" is too far removed from the action of sketching. It is confusing whether the person was in watercolor. Better would be:

> Correct: I sketched the Eiffel Tower in watercolor when I was in Paris.

You should also be cautious about misplacing single words. The words in the group that tend to be misplaced include *nearly, only, even, almost, exactly, hardly* etc. and should come immediately before the word they modify. For example:

Misplaced modifier: My portfolio nearly has 40 pieces in it.

Correct: My portfolio has nearly 40 pieces in it.

In the following sentences, moving the modifier creates different meaning.

Only Megan took studio class last semester.

Megan took only studio class last semester

Megan took studio class only last semester.

The first sentence means that Megan, among others, was the only person to take studio class. The second sentence indicates that studio class was the single class Megan took, and the third sentence means that Megan had taken class very recently.

CONCLUSION

Statements of design philosophy and manifestos are architecture's most unique writing genres. The audience for one's design philosophy may be either internal or external, but the manifesto is almost exclusively intended for an audience of other architects. The statement of design philosophy should be a reflective piece—it is evidence of the author's ability to productively look inward and take stock of herself as a design professional. The rhetorical standards of the manifesto, however, are much different: they require a distinctly artistic component in the writing itself, which would be out of place in almost any other writing genre. The temptation to overcome in the manifesto is that of making broad generalizations that cannot be given strong illustration or that respond to no situation in particular. By placing your manifesto's genesis in your knowledge of architecture history and in response to what others have written, you will have gone a long way toward avoiding what would appear to readers as high-minded banality. When done correctly, the statement of design philosophy will help the author's process of self-discovery as an architect. A good manifesto is inherently gregarious: it will help launch a new line of communication with your peers. In both cases, you will in effect be making the statement: "Here I stand."

1. Think back to when you started architecture school. What did you think architecture was at that time? What do you think it is now? How did your ideas about it change?

2. Choose either Le Corbusier's or Venturi's manifesto and model your own after one of them.

exercises

THESES

Thesis work in an architecture curriculum will typically fall into one of two categories: the design thesis and the written thesis. The design thesis is an original, largely self-generated investigation that takes the form of a typical design project presentation. It differs from a design studio project in the depth of investigation and in the thoroughness with which the investigator is expected to know the literature on the topic. Topics suitable for a design thesis may include such investigations as:

- The design implications of a new technology applied to a building type.
- Possible architectural solutions to new social problems.
- Design guidelines for a historic district.

The more academically traditional written thesis will likely take one of two basic forms:

- An original investigation into a design issue.
- A new interpretation of already known facts.

The first involves ascertaining and explaining the facts of a heretofore poorly understood or ill-defined situation. In the second type, a body of knowledge—sociology, say, or deep ecology, or solid state mechanics—is the resource to better understand an existing situation: problems in professional practice, dead shopping centers, heat conduction through buildings. Neither form of investigation is easier than the other. The success of the first depends on uncovering or generating something new: a new opinion survey perhaps, or sensor data, and this new information should conform to the data-gathering standards of the sciences or the social sciences. The second type of investigation doesn't necessarily require gathering new data, but to be able to apply the conceptual resources of one discipline to architecture requires a sound working knowledge of the literature of not one, but two disciplines.

No matter which form a written thesis takes, it will be written for a highly demanding, knowledgeable, and predictably critical insider audience: the thesis committee. The combined demands of creating an original investigation and writing for a highly critical audience can be a frightening prospect but they must not be allowed to lead to writing paralysis. As with any potentially intimidating task, the proven technique for managing thesis writing is to break it down into sensible parts. In this chapter, the process of thesis writing is divided into a series of steps augmented by suggestions to help keep you efficient and productive. Though at times it might seem otherwise, your thesis readers actually do want to see you succeed, but only if your work meets their standards. Engaging your readers in detailed conversation at the outset regarding their standards can save much anguish later. Do not just assume that you and they are on the same wavelength in this important matter.

Keeping the writing process in mind is especially important when working on a large project such as a thesis. Preparation, drafting, revising, polishing, and editing are all parts of the writing process—they don't always occur in that order and they can be recursive; for example, you may have to go back to planning after revising if you decide to add more material or discover that you must develop an idea further. Happily, it all begins with an activity any architecture student should be thoroughly comfortable with by now: keeping a journal.

PREPARATORY WORK

We discussed the design journal in Chapter 2. Keeping a notebook or journal is as important at this juncture in your architecture curriculum as it was earlier. One of the criteria of a successful thesis is originality. In order to get to an original question, you will need to do quite a bit of exploring of ideas. Keeping a research notebook will help you localize your thoughts and provide a space to reflect on your ideas, which will help you narrow your focus.

Obviously, both in the design thesis and in both types of written thesis, you will be reading a lot and it is easy to forget what you have read. Try to write a longish paragraph immediately upon finishing each article, book, or essay you read. The paragraph should be more than a mere summary; it should record ideas that the article or book generates in your mind while reading. If the reading generated no ideas (questions, agreement, rebuttals, similarities to other authors, place in the literature), then it was probably worthless to your thesis. What a pity: time is limited. Make each reading count! Disciplining yourself to write *something* about each reading is a great way to improve recall and to practice the arts of summarizing and condensing what you have read. At the same time, use the journal to begin the crucial task of keeping track of and organizing your sources. You will need to find the system that works best for you, but a notebook can assist you as a place to keep notes about sources. Below are some key suggestions for working with sources.

Create a system of organization for your notes that includes a consistent form in which you record them. This will save time later as you are reviewing and writing passages based on these notes.

When you take notes, be sure to record the source information. This will help you remember where ideas originated and it will help as you write your bibliography. This is one of the best pieces of advices we can give. Keeping this information organized and available early on in the process will prevent unnecessary and frantic work at the end of the thesis writing process. Resist the temptation, due to the informality of the journal, to only record the author's name and the title. Take the extra minute to record the complete bibliographic information you will need at the end. This will include not only author and title, but also city, publisher, and date and, for any quotation, a page number. If the source is a journal article, record the page number, volume number, and date. If the source is from the internet, *be sure to record the date you accessed the page.* On a research project of any length, some of the web pages you used will be rearranged, updated, pulled or shut down. These changes can be a major source of anxiety and confusion when an important quotation no longer exists in cyberspace.

On a similar note: be sure to put quotation marks around words that come from the author. This will help you avoid the possible embarrassment or worse of plagiarism. One note about quoting: use quotes *sparingly* throughout your thesis.

As part of your note taking, you will want to record substantive information as well:

- What is the main idea of this piece?
- What methods has this author used to make an argument?
- How is this piece similar to or different from other sources?
- Are there weaknesses in the argument?

In earlier times, students used 3 × 5 index cards to record this information. In more recent times, convenient electronic systems such as EndNote have improved the ease of notetaking and serve the same purpose. Here is an example of how you might organize your information based on an index card format on the page in your electronic document.

```
Author name (Last, First, Middle Initial):
Title of work:
Publisher/Publication date:
Inclusive Page numbers (if a journal article, volume
and issue number):
Main Idea/Summary:
Methods:
Similarities/Differences:
Weaknesses/Strengths:
```

It is better to keep more notes than you think you will need. A source that you think may not be relevant at the beginning of your process could be important later on and you don't want to have to go back to the library to recover sources.

As you are reading through sources for your thesis, there are other substantive concerns you should attend to:

- What terminology is being used by the author, and how does that individual use those terms?
- What kind of methodology is the author using? What are the weaknesses and strengths in methodology?
- What do others say about the source? Is the source going to be one that helps corroborate your theoretical stance, or one you must overcome? (You need both kinds.)
- What patterns do you see in the sources? Are there relationships?
- What gaps or omissions are there in the sources?
- How closely aligned with your topic is this source?
- Is the source material current and relevant?

Doing this kind of analytical work as you read your sources will help you develop you topic and your argument for your thesis.

In addition to providing a location to begin recording quotes, ideas, and sources, the notebook is also an excellent venue for exploring possible thesis topics. Establishing a suitable topic is the single most difficult task in thesis writing. This task is so formidable that often a thesis preparation course is required just so the student can enter the thesis writing class prepared to move forward. The difficulty usually takes the form of settling on a topic of interest narrow enough that it can be addressed in one semester yet open enough that not everything interesting to be discovered on the topic has already been said. Perhaps you are fascinated by the influence of Frank Lloyd Wright's Oak Park Prairie School architecture on architecture in other parts of the mid-Western United States. This is an already well-trod topic. Do you think you can find a previously obscure area of influence? Can you contextualize the work in a region to find unexpected associations?

Is it technologically different from the Oak Park work? Have the artistic aims changed as the style is retranslated elsewhere? In other words, to turn an interest into a thesis, you must be able to reformulate that interest into a sharpened question around which your investigation hovers. Reaching this juncture takes many iterations and much refinement. As you progress through your preparatory readings, potential topics should begin to suggest themselves so it is only convenient and sensible to freely mix reading notes with topic generation ideas.

DRAFTING

The actual writing process begins with the drafting. Some find this process pleasant and easy, but for many it is very difficult to do. This is a bigger writing project than you have ever tackled before and it is a good idea to develop strategies that will help you succeed.

Here are a few suggestions:

- Find a place that is comfortable for your writing. It helps if this space is only used for the writing and not other activities.
- By extension, if you write at the keyboard, you may want to close email, Facebook, or other distractions that may pop up on your screen.
- Be sure to have the tools you need handy in your space—a computer, pens, paper etc.
- Determine the best time of day to get your writing done. For some people, morning is when they feel the freshest and ready to tackle new work. For others, nighttime yields more quiet and better thinking time. Each of us has our own rhythms—find yours.
- Write *regularly*. It is much easier to finish a big project if there is regular attention to the work. A daily, regularly scheduled time is going to help you make steady progress. You will not be able to finish a thesis without paying regular attention to the writing.

- Find a rhythm for reading and writing. Do you read first and then write or vice versa?
- Finally, time on task is the most important piece of advice we can offer. The more time you have the pen in your hand or your fingers on the keyboard, the more words you will get down on the paper.
- If you are self-disciplined enough, try to leave yourself a small task to begin the next writing session with. This will help get your mind back into the subject after it has rested. For example, say you are writing a thesis about the distinctive cultural attributes of contemporary Japanese architecture and you need to type in some quotes. Leave that relatively rote task for the next session. You will be able to dive directly back into the work without the delay of having to ask and answer: "Now where was I?"

To begin the drafting process you may want to start with an outline of the thesis. Make the outline as detailed as you can at this point in the process. At the top, state the topic. See the graphic below for a possible format for the outline. Fill out as much as you can at this point.

Topic: Here is where you state your topic/idea

Introduction: Contains your statement of purpose and your research questions.

Section 1

Section 2

Section 3

Section X

Sections 1 through X are the major points of your argument. Eventually, these sections will constitute the major portion of your thesis and include your sources materials.

Methodological issues: Contains the methodology of your approach to your argument.

Summary of your argument, implications of your research, future directions for research.

In order to fill in the sections that relate to your argument, you will want to organize your notes. Your notes about the gaps, methodological strengths and weaknesses of various sources and their relationship to your topic can all help you to organize your notes. Organize them by theme. You will find that the time you spend with your sources at this point in the process will be time well spent. The first draft tends to focus paragraphs around the source information rather than around the ideas of the writer. By organizing your sources around themes initially, you will be better able to organize your writing by your ideas and the points of your argument. What constitutes a theme within a thesis? Themes can take on widely different forms, but common themes organize according to such customary topics as technological developments, recognizable historic periods, distinctive problems that must be solved, points of view provided by different authors or groups of authors, or related building types. In the paper mentioned earlier on the subject of cultural influences on contemporary Japanese architecture, one might organize around themes of Eastern and Western cultural influences, traditional and persistent cultural influences from within Japan itself, the influence of modernity, and finally how it all becomes synthesized within the work of exemplary architects. It is not too difficult to imagine these themes ultimately becoming chapters.

This brings up the concept that themes must have a certain alikeness or symmetry to them. Think of them as if you would place them as a series of terms within a sentence. It would be a strange series indeed that included architect Tadao Ando, the Meiji Period, the city of Nara, and the aesthetic concept wabi because these topics, as interesting as each may be, lack the necessary alikeness to provide complementary, yet mutually exclusive, repositories for your notes and ideas. One would be much better served to, say, choose an exemplary set of architects to illustrate different aesthetic concepts, or conversely, a set of aesthetic concepts as the themes which are then illustrated in the work of various architects. Naturally, these themes should be allowed to evolve as your understanding of the subject grows and matures. But they should never lose their quality of alikeness.

Once the notes are organized, you can refine your outline with topic and subtopics or start writing in paragraph form. Either strategy is equally valid. The point is that, either way, you are filling in your argument with the details and subtleties that relate to the major ideas expressed in the outline. Especially important in a work of theory, but also a valid suggestion in a work generating new knowledge, is to align each outline topic and subtopic with at least one author or reading source. Though conceivably you have subtopics of such startling originality that nothing of importance has ever been written on it, it is unlikely. Allow the argument from that source to inform your exposition of the subtopic.

As with all writing projects, your outline and your prose will work together and change as you write. The process of writing does not merely set down ideas already fully formed in the mind. Do not wait for that to happen! The writing itself will help you work through your ideas as long as you are willing to revise.

REVISING

As in design revisions, each thesis revision should bring you closer to the simplest and most direct possible expression of your ideas. Do not hesitate to disassemble and reassemble. There is something to be learned from each iteration. As you read through your draft and are getting ready to revise your thesis, you will want to ask the following questions.

■ Have I provided a clear statement of the topic? Not too broad or too narrow?

Engage your architecture audience by introducing your topic in a familiar way that doesn't evoke all of architectural history or theory or practice (whatever approach you are taking), but also doesn't leave the reader room for confusion about your topic. Remember, you are writing for a knowledgeable reader. You should not have to explain elemental terms. At the thesis level, you are dissecting and assembling highly technical or highly abstract topics for an insider audience. Your ability to handle the language appropriate to the topic will be one measure of your overall competence. As always, aim for precision.

■ Does my introduction express to the reader WHY this topic is important for architecture?

By this time in the writing process after spending hours and hours with it, you know why your topic is important. However, having gone so deeply into the process, it is easy to have failed to make it clear to the audience. Re-read the introduction for the presence of the "why." Why is the topic important? What should the reader expect to gain from reading the entire thesis? You may want to ask a friend or classmate to read for the why. For example, to simply assert that it should be "interesting" to better understand the cultural influences on contemporary Japanese architecture would not be enough, however true that may be. For a thesis, one would want to be able to assert, for example, the relevance for better understanding the malleability and durability of culture in general provided by this study. However, one must beware of making excessive claims of importance. Seldom would a thesis completely overturn existing ways of understanding a topic. Rarely would a committee expect a thesis to provide an entirely new theoretical perspective. No one expects a thesis to provide a scientific or technological breakthrough. It is enough if a thesis provides a new perspective on a familiar topic, fills in a gap or adds to the periphery of a body of knowledge, makes some connections between hitherto disparate disciplines, gathers and organizes scattered information for the use of subsequent scholars, makes a compelling argument for reconsideration of a sidelined or neglected topic, or records and generalizes from a series of experiments. Any committee would be glad to read theses that did these things. Much better that the "why" of a thesis be quite narrow than be so broad it is bland.

■ Have I highlighted certain studies or sources that are important in their relationship to my topic?

There are several reasons for including outside sources in a thesis, not the least of which is demonstrating that you have read enough to know that you are creating new knowledge. You help demonstrate this when you let the reader know what sources are more or less important in relation to your argument. Group these sources according to classes of importance for your topic. State which sources are the subject standards and which contain narrower but compelling information. If the thesis is a work of theory, then a brief discussion of the theoretical provenance is a must. How do you know when you have read enough to begin drafting? Here's a good rule of thumb: when in subsequent readings you encounter references to other authors you have already read, then you can be fairly well assured that you have a grasp of the scope of the relevant literature. But if, as you read, you keep encountering references to other sources with which you have no familiarity, then this is a good indication that you must keep up the reading. A good thesis advisor should be able to help with a reading list.

■ Have I included all of the relevant sources for my argument?

You do not need to know every single source ever written, but you also want to be sure you have included the relevant sources to your topic. You may want to check back at your research notes and be sure that you have included all of the sources you thought you needed initially. If you find that you have omitted a source that you have reason to think your readers will find salient, this creates a problem that must be addressed either by including that source or else by explaining why that source may be ignored. Ignoring relevant sources is a potential minefield for a thesis writer's relationship with his or her committee. The very source you have no use for may be a committee member's pet favorite. Much better to face the situation head on than try an end run.

■ Have I provided a good roadmap of my argument for the reader?

You may want to go through and outline what you actually have in your draft. After outlining, determine whether you can follow the flow of your argument from the outline. If not, do you need to add or delete sections that might assist in the flow of your argument? Alternatively, try to write a one-paragraph synopsis of the argument. If this comes easily, wonderful! If not, it is an indication that the argument is not yet clear in your own mind. Your argument is too complex for a one-paragraph synopsis you say? Try going to any scholarly journal. No paper is too technical or too complex for a synopsis. It is required. The synopsis is a scholar's stock-in-trade.

■ **Are the methods I used to collect and present data clear to the reader? Have I addressed any weaknesses in my methods?**

Because the written thesis is an academic document, it is important that the reader knows *how* you arrived at your conclusions. Be sure that the methods by which you came to your assertions and conclusions are clearly stated. Do not shy away from stating your work's limitations. Better to be aware of them, and perhaps even more important, to let your committee readers know that you are aware of them. Modesty and evident self-awareness are much appreciated qualities in a thesis.

■ **Do I conclude the thesis with a reasonable conclusion, implications for the field, and suggestions for further research in the field?**

Be sure that conclusions emerge out of your argument and methods. Making new claims in the conclusion that have not been previously supported leaves the reader confused and, often, unconvinced of the writer's credibility. The reader will also want you to re-engage the why question—how does this work relate to the larger field of architecture? In addition, where do you think this research could lead? Pointing out future directions for subsequent research serves two purposes. It shows the fertility of the subject, and it demonstrates that you are aware of the limits of what you have so far achieved.

■ **Does each of my paragraphs contain one main idea and support for that idea?**

In working with so much material and so many ideas, writers often succumb to packing many ideas in one space. This can be confusing to the audience. While some ideas and connections between ideas may seem evident to you, they may not be for the reader. Having clearly organized paragraphs that have good main ideas articulated can help you help the reader traverse the terrain of your argument.

■ Are there transitions between sentences, paragraphs, and sections of my thesis?

We discussed sentence transitions and their importance in Chapter 3. In addition, having transitions between paragraphs is as important as having a main idea for each paragraph. Make the connections for the reader. In a document as long as a thesis, transition paragraphs may also be necessary to help the reader understand how major sections fit together.

■ Have I used appropriate documentation conventions to introduce and discuss my source materials?

Attention to detail is important. Be sure to check and recheck all references and other documentation details. This may come as a surprise, but many scholars actually read the bibliography first! The bibliography says much about an author's theoretical stance, approach to the topic, and critical influences. So do not assume that it will be read casually or inattentively. What may seem initially as fanatical attention to detail will become customary, and will pay-off.

FEEDBACK

In most university situations, students work closely with their thesis advisors as the thesis writing progresses. Expect to receive feedback from your advisor and others on your written document. When you are submitting a draft and then reviewing the comments made on your drafts consider the following:

• Proofread before you hand your draft to a reviewer for feedback! Do not feel that you must wait for feedback before beginning to polish your draft. Write at your best even for preliminary feedback.

- Expect that your advisor can only comment on what you have on the paper, not on what is still in your head.
- If the reader is confused, the responsibility is yours to clear up the confusion.
- Read for the conceptual and structural comments on your ideas first. Address the sentence level comments later even though these may be the easiest to address.
- If you change ideas, this may entail changing sentences, so it is more efficient to deal with content and organization first.
- Ask for clarification—especially if you have gotten conflicting feedback from two different sources.

Remember that the feedback you receive is designed to make your thesis better. The time your advisor spends reading and commenting on your drafts is precious and she has put effort into the process. Respond to feedback keeping these points in mind. Your advisor does not consider any of her comments to be "throwaways." You must respond to every point your thesis advisor makes, even if only to explain a lack of adjustment.

DOCUMENTATION STYLE

Most universities have standard guidelines for formatting and documentation. Be sure to check these parameters before you get started. Using these guidelines from the beginning of the process will prevent costly time spent at the end when you are doing final revisions to your thesis.

FINALLY

Writing a thesis can seem to be a daunting task. However, if you approach the writing as you might the design process, you will find writing a thesis is much like designing a building with similar pleasures and pains, rewards and costs.

Notice how Matthew Frederick's *101 Things I Learned in Architecture School*[1] apply equally well to the writing process:

> #14 Architecture begins with an idea . . . Without underlying ideas informing their buildings, architects are merely *space planners.*

Writing begins with an idea . . . Without underlying ideas informing their writing, writers are merely word movers. *Your journal is a place to explore ideas and dream ideas—use it to add interest and substance to your writing. Within your text, make sure each paragraph contains an idea and, then, corresponds to a single idea.*

> #17 The more specific a design idea is the greater its appeal is likely to be. Being nonspecific in an effort to appeal to everyone usually results in reaching no one. But drawing upon a specific observation, poignant statement, ironic point, witty reflection, intellectual connection, political argument, or idiosyncratic belief in a creative work can help you create environments others will identify in their own way.

The more specific a writing idea is, the greater its appeal. Being nonspecific in an effort to appeal to everyone usually results in reaching no one. But drawing upon a specific observation, poignant statement, ironic point, witty reflection, intellectual connection, political argument, or idiosyncratic belief in a creative work can help you create environments others will identify in their own way. *When you speak in abstractions, you lose the reader. You will want to use specifics to get and maintain the attention of the reader. This gives a creative work handles for observers and readers to imaginatively grasp the work.*

> #18 Any design decision should be justified in at least two ways.

Any writing decision should be justified in at least two ways. *As you write, think about why you are making the decisions you do as you go. Ask yourself questions such as: If I say it this way, what are the implications? This is the essence of the integration process in both architectural design and in writing. Otherwise, one creates a series of ideas, each of which is ultimately a dead end.*

> #19 Draw hierarchically. When drawing in any medium, never work at "100% level of detail" from one end of the sheet toward the other . . . Instead, start with the most general elements of the composition and work gradually toward the more specific aspects of it . . . Evaluate your success continually, making local adjustments in the context of the entire sheet.

Write hierarchically. *We have emphasized this approach in this chapter: outline and then work with the details; adjust your details to the larger picture as you go. This cannot be stressed enough. Improving the logic and flow of a creative work is a constant process.*

> #25 Use your *parti* as a guidepost in designing the many aspects of a building.

Use your thesis statement as a guidepost in writing the sentences and paragraphs of your paper. *By using your thesis as a guidepost (which may also be adjusted as you write—see the previous entry), you tend to stay true to your vision. This is what gives a creative work discipline; what establishes the criteria for including or discarding elements.*

> #26 Good designers are fast on their feet.

Good writers are fast on their feet. *They are able to assess the writing situation and, based on exigencies, make changes to both the direction of their writing and to the overall thesis, if need be.*

> #27 Soft ideas, soft lines; hard ideas, hard lines.

Soft ideas, soft words; hard ideas, hard words. *If you are trying to make a clear and straightforward point, you don't want to use qualifying language like* perhaps, *or* inserting a modal like *could. However, you would use these if you are trying to provide a tempered perspective (see the Language Conventions section of Chapter 3 for examples of this). Understand the level of abstraction at which you are working, and make the language appropriate.*

#28 A good designer isn't afraid to throw away a good idea.

A good writer isn't afraid to throw away a good idea. *Sometimes, we get attached to a good idea, but that idea gets in the way of the overall purpose, organization or flow of the writing. We need to be able to recognize when this happens and let that idea go. However, you can save it. It is money in the bank. Be confident you will find a use for it eventually and be glad of it.*

#29 Being process-oriented, not product-driven, is the most important and difficult skill for a designer to develop.

Being process-oriented, not product-driven, is the most important and difficult skill for a writer to develop. *In this section, Frederick lists the characteristics of being process oriented, which translate to writing:*

- *Understand your topic*
- *Don't force the writing where it doesn't fit*
- *Don't fall in love with ideas that might interfere with the success of the writing*
- *Know when to change directions*
- *Be able to go any direction without anxiety*
- *Work at both abstract and concrete levels*
- *Always ask "What if?"*

And we would like to add: Recall E.B. White's "The best writing is rewriting!"[2]

#32 The most creative problem solvers engage in a process of meta-thinking or "thinking about the thinking." Meta-thinking means that you are aware of *how* you are thinking as you are *doing* the thinking. Meta-thinkers engage in a continual internal dialogue of testing, stretching, criticizing and directing their thought processes.

The most creative writers engage in a process of meta-thinking or "thinking about thinking" OR we could even say "thinking about writing." *Continually test how you are doing the writing and thinking about the writing. Stretch yourself to review and write about the writing and thinking processes you are engaging in. This is also related to the importance of the thesis statement in #25: develop the discipline to mentally stand back from the work from time to time to gain a sense of the overall contours of your argument.*

#33. If you wish to imbue an architectural space or element with a particular quality, make sure that quality is really there.

If you wish to imbue your writing with a particular quality, be sure that quality is there. *If you want your writing to reflect complex thinking, be sure that your writing is at a suitably high level. Asserting a thing to be true or present and actually making it present are two different things.*

#39 & 40 A static composition appears to be at rest.
A dynamic composition encourages the eye to explore

A static piece of writing contains static words. A dynamic piece of writing contains dynamic words. *Using dynamic words and verbs will engage the reader's eye and imagination. See Chapter 7 for a discussion of active and stative verbs.*

IN CONCLUSION

The thesis is likely the first occasion to demonstrate that you are ready to go beyond the professional status quo—that you have joined the community of inquirers seeking to mold the discipline and improve the built environment. It is a *summa* moment in a career and in a life. It draws on everything you have learned to date, demands subtlety of thought, and requires powerful, clear expression. All the previously discussed genre, writing process, subject matter, and rhetorical knowledge gained in the earlier years will be brought to bear on the successfully executed thesis. Tremble before the size of the task if you must, but only briefly, because writing well is a skill like countless others you have already mastered in your progress toward becoming an architect. Take a deep breath. Start organizing your thoughts. Have confidence. *Go Forth! Write!*

NOTES

1 HOW (AND WHY) ARCHITECTS WRITE

1   Ludwig Wittgenstein, *Philosophical Investigations*, trans. G.E.M.
    Anscombe (Englewood Cliffs, NJ: Prentice Hall, 1958), 108.
2   Peter Medway, "Language, Learning and 'Communication' in an
    Architects' Office," *English in Education* 28 (1994): 6.
3   Peter Medway and Richard Andrews, "Building with Words: Discourse
    in an Architects' Office," *Carleton Papers in Applied Language Studies*
    9 (1992): 23.
4   Peter Medway, "Writing and Design in Architectural Education," in
    Transitions: Writing in Academic and Workplace Settings, ed. Patrick
    Dias and Anthony Paré (Cresskill, NJ: Hampton Press, 2000), 117.
5   Peter Medway, "Rhetoric and Architecture," in *Learning to Argue
    In Higher Education*, ed. Sally Mitchell and Richard Andrews
    (Portsmouth, NH: Boynton/Cook Heinemann, 2000), 36.

2 DESIGN JOURNALS

1   Donald Schön, *The Reflective Practitioner: How Professionals Think in
    Action* (London: Ashgate, 1983), 76.
2   Matthew Frederick, *101 Things I Learned In Architecture School*
    (Cambridge, MA: The MIT Press, 2007), 99.
3   Sue Grafton, "The Use of the Journal in Writing the Private Eye
    Novel," in *Writers and Their Notebooks*, ed. Diana Raab (Columbia,
    SC: The University of South Carolina Press, 2010), 9.
4   Moh'd Bilbeisi, *Graphic Journaling* (Dubuque, IA: Kendall/Hunt
    Publishing, 2009), 3.
5   Andrea Ponsi, *Florence: A Map of Perceptions* (Charlottesville, VA:
    University of Virginia Press, 2010), 80.

3 HISTORY TERM PAPERS

1 Michael Rabens, "ARCH 4173 – Skyscrapers" (research paper guidelines, Oklahoma State University, 2010), 1.

2 Elizabeth Kryder-Reid, "'Perennially New': Santa Barbara and the Origins of the California Mission Garden," *Journal of the Society of Architectural Historians* 69, 3 (2010): 378.

3 Travis McLain, "Masonic Skyscrapers: An Examination" (research paper, Oklahoma State University, 2010), 2.

4 Kryder-Reid, "Perennially New," 394.

5 Edward Tufte, *Beautiful Evidence* (Cheshire, Connecticut: Graphics Press LLC, 2006), 9.

6 Ibid.

7 Kryder-Reid, "Perennially New," 395.

8 Ibid., 384.

9 Ibid., 378.

10 Ibid., 378.

11 Ibid., 379.

12 Meredith L. Clausen, "The Ecole des Beaux-Arts: Toward a Gendered History," *Journal of the Society of Architectural Historians* 69, 2 (2010): 154.

13 Charles Anthony Stewart, "The First Vaulted Churches in Cyprus," *Journal of the Society of Architectural Historians* 69, 2 (2010): 183.

14 The University of Chicago, *The Chicago Manual of Style*, 16th ed. (Chicago: The University of Chicago Press, 2010), 626.

15 Kryder-Reid, "Perennially New," 379.

16 Ibid., 379.

17 Ibid., 378.

18 Ibid., 378

19 Ken Hyland, *Metadiscourse* (New York: Continuum, 2005), 218–224.

20 Kryder-Reid, "Perennially New," 378.

21 Ibid., 399–400.

22 Vincent Michael, "Expressing the Modern: Barry Byrne in 1920s Europe," *Journal of the Society of Architectural Historians* 69, 4 (2010): 534.

4 PROJECT DESCRIPTIONS

1 William McDonough + Partners, "Greenbridge," accessed November 15, 2010, http://www.mcdonoughpartners.com/projects/view/greenbridge.

2   Peter Eisenman, "Visions' Unfolding: Architecture in the Age of Electronic Media," in *The Invisible in Architecture*, ed. Ole Bouman and Roemer van Toorn (London: Academy Editions, 1994), 147.

3   William McDonough + Partners, "Greenbridge."

4   Peter Eisenman, "Project Descriptions and Gallery," *Stanford Presidential Lectures and Symposia in the Humanities and Arts*, last modified 1998, http://prelectur.stanford.edu/lecturers/eisenman/projects.html#aronoff.

5   William McDonough + Partners, "Greenbridge."

6   Eisenman, "Project Descriptions and Gallery."

7   Ralph Erskine quoted in Richard Eden, *Clare Hall: The Origins and Development of a College for Advanced Study* (Cambridge: Fellows of Clare Hall, 2009), 168.

8   Nicholas Ray, *Cambridge Architecture: A Concise Guide* (Cambridge: Cambridge University Press, 1994), 114.

6   BUSINESS DOCUMENTS

1   Joe M. Powell, *The New Competitiveness in Design and Construction: 12 Strategies That Will Drive the 21st-century's Most Successful Firms* (New York: Wiley, 2008).

2   "Profile," Pei Cobb Freed & Partners, accessed November 15, 2010, http://www.pcf-p.com/a/f/.

3   "About BNIM," BNIM, accessed November 15, 2010, http://www.bnim.com/press/quick-facts/about-bnim.

4   Callison, "Flatiron Crossing," accessed November 15, 2010, http://www.callison.com/portfolio/index.cfm?display=project&Project_ID=27.

5   "Ad Agency," RBA, accessed November 15, 2010, http://www.randybrownarchitects.com/project/ad-agency.

6   Ibid.

7   STATEMENTS OF DESIGN PHILOSOPHY AND MANIFESTOS

1   Gavin Knight, *Monograph: Selected Works 2005–2011* (Self-published, 2011), 1.

2   Bethany Waterman, *Pettia: A Reflection on the First 5 Years* (Self-published, 2011), 4.

3   Oxford English Dictionary, "Manifesto, N.," accessed January 23, 2011, http://www.oed.com/view/Entry/113499?rskey=Fh3qQW&result=1&isAdvanced=false#eid.

4 Le Corbusier, *Toward a New Architecture*, trans. Frederick Etchells (New York: Dover Publications, 1986), 269.

5 Robert Venturi, *Complexity and Contradiction in Architecture* (New York: The Museum of Modern Art, 1966), 22–23.

6 Charles Jencks, "The Volcano and the Tablet," in *Theories and Manifestoes of Contemporary Architecture*, 2nd ed., ed. Charles Jencks and Karl Kropf (Hoboken, NJ: Wiley-Academy, 2006), 7.

7 Ibid., 3.

8 Ibid., 2.

9 Ibid., 7.

10 Rem Koolhaas, "Junkspace," in *Constructing a New Agenda: Architectural Theory 1993–2009*, ed. Krista Sykes (New York: Princeton Architectural Press, 2010), 136–137.

11 Jencks, "Volcano and Tablet," 6–7.

12 Louis Kahn, "Order is," in *Programs and Manifestoes on 20th-Century Architecture*, ed. Ulrich Conrads, trans. Michael Bullock (Cambridge, MA: The MIT Press, 1970), 169.

13 Congress for the New Urbanism, "Charter of the New Urbanism," in Sykes, *Constructing a New Agenda*, 65–68.

14 Kahn, "Order is," 169–170.

15 Sykes, *Constructing a New Agenda*, 73–74.

16 Deborah Berke, "Thoughts on the Everyday," in Conrads, *Programs and Manifestoes*, 73–74.

17 Ibid., 74–75.

18 Ibid., 75.

19 Kahn, "Order is," 169.

20 Ibid., 170.

21 Berke, "Thoughts on the Everyday," 75.

8 THESES

1 Matthew Frederick, *101 Things I Learned In Architecture School* (Cambridge, MA: The MIT Press, 2007).

2 William Strunk and E.B. White, *The Elements of Style*, 4th ed. (New York: Longman, 1999).

INDEX

Numbers in *italics* refer to figures.